Wall Street on a Shoestring

WALL STREET ON A SHOESTRING

CLARE LA PLANTE

AVON BOOKS NEW YORK

NOTE TO READER:

All information contained herein was current at the time of publication. All readers are advised that they should perform any extra work necessary to make sure any investing they do is appropriate for their particular circumstances. Investing is a personal decision, and neither the author nor the publisher are responsible for any reader's investing decisions or their outcomes.

AVON BOOKS, INC.
1350 Avenue of the Americas
New York, New York 10019

Interior design by Rhea Braunstein
Published by arrangement with the author
Visit our website at **http://www.AvonBooks.com**
ISBN: 0-380-79520-5

Library of Congress Cataloging in Publication Data:
La Plante, Clare.
Wall Street on a shoestring / Clare La Plante.
p. cm.
Includes bibliographical references and index.
1. Finance, Personal. 2. Investments. 3. Retirement income.
4. Mutual funds. 5. Dividend reinvestment. 6. Investment clubs.
I. Title.
HG179.L2 1998 98-25576
332.024—dc21 CIP

First Avon Books Trade Paperback Printing: October 1998

Printed in the U.S.A.

OPM 10 9 8 7 6 5 4 3 2 1

Contents

Acknowledgments

I benefited immensely by essential advice and assistance in the writing of this book. First, I want to thank Tom Siedell, managing editor of *Your Money* magazine for his encouragement and expertise. I also want to thank his colleagues Dennis Fertig and Deborah Rogus, and *Consumers Digest/Your Money* publishers Arthur and Randy Weber for giving me opportunities in journalism.

I also want to thank my sister, Catherine La Plante-Klauke, for her discerning eye and patience in reading drafts of the book. My brother-in-law, Joe Klauke, contributed his organizational skills and legal advice. Michael Allaway, read the manuscript with the eye of a professional. Sonny Ginsburg contributed contract law expertise and *Nashville Skyline*.

Dave Cox of the Chicago Trust Corporation brought investment insight, plus some great charts. Darryl Reed of Moneyminds brought the $5-a-day investor to life.

To all of these collaborators—thank you. Finally, I want to thank my editor, Stephen S. Power, for a great book idea and the opportunity to bring it to life.

Introduction

Much ingenuity with a little money is vastly more profitable and amusing than much money without ingenuity.
—Arnold Bennett

What does $5 a day mean to you?

A quick lunch out? A few magazines on the train ride home? A cafe latte and a croissant on your morning walk?

What does $971,103 mean? A vacation home in the Florida Keys? A retirement filled with security? Private schooling for your children?

Why do I ask?

Consider this proposition: Invest $5 a day, every day, for the next forty years. If you take this challenge, and assuming the stock market average of a 10 percent return, your $5 a day would turn into $971,103. That's nearly $1,000,000 for forsaking daily habits that you might want to forsake anyway. Even if you saved $5 a day for only thirty years, with a 10 percent return you're looking at $362,067—after depositing only $56,575. A 15 percent return, a possibility depending on your investment choices and risk tolerance, would net you $1,330,259.

Not a bad deal, you think. What's the catch?

Actually, there are several. First, the human race in general, and Americans in particular, are not primed to think of the future. Immediate gratification is, well, more gratifying. Several years of diligent saving without big results can lead to frustration. Unless you've experienced it firsthand, it's difficult to appreciate the power of compound interest. So you need patience.

Investing also requires commitment and discipline. You may really miss those daily lattes. Financial limits may feel like life limitations. You may ponder the trade-offs. And, after all, we should live life to the fullest. You could be hit by lightning tomorrow, right?

You could also live to be ninety. So it makes sense to think ahead, and to plan for your future. Smart investing usually means spending less, staying out of debt, and paying attention to things such as taxes. It also requires financial consciousness. Americans are taught less about how to save and invest than they are the intricacies of a field goal or the fastest way to apply for credit.

And that's too bad. Personal investing is relatively easy to understand, and it can make the difference between a life of struggle and a life of comfort. Nearly everyone has the ability—and need—to save and invest. In fact, some of the country's best investors have been immigrants who were learning a new language and a new trade while investing for the future.

Saving begets saving—and other good things. Not only do you acquire money but you also acquire responsibility and a sense of pride. Your mother was right—you do reap what you sow; a penny saved really is a penny earned; and anything worth having is worth working for.

This book is for both the novice and the experienced investor. It's for anyone serious about acquiring financial habits that lead to mastery. Financial stability is about freedom: freedom to live how you want to live and to do the things you want to do. Few things are more exciting than assuming control over your life, and few things allow this sense of control as readily as financial stability.

This book is not a panacea; we would be charlatans if we claimed it would solve all your problems and make you rich overnight. Instead, it is a commonsense guide to creating an investing plan for yourself that feels comfortable and accessible.

Why did we choose $5? Because some of us have traveled Europe on that amount per day, and most of us can cut that from our daily spending. It can also become an amazing amount of money when you invest it over the long term. Really, you're not choosing $5; you're choosing that $971,103.

This book will teach you what you need to know to invest your hard-earned $5 wisely. And you'll learn that the rules of investing are most effective when you apply them to your own life and values. As Benjamin Franklin said, "The advantage of money is in its use."

ONE

Getting Started

I've got all the money I'll ever need
if I die by four o'clock.
—Henny Youngman

When it comes to investing, getting started is the hard part. Where do you go? Whom do you call? How do you know which investments to choose—stocks, bonds, mutual funds, CDs, money markets? How do you know when to buy and when to sell? And even if you can figure all that out, how do you get the money that you need to invest? After all, it takes money to make money, right?

Well, not exactly. It takes commitment, discipline, and patience to make money in investing. You need the commitment to stay with an investment plan; the discipline to pay yourself first; and the patience to realize that effective investing takes time.

And investing begins with saving. But let's face it. Saving is not the American way. This wasn't always the case, however. Americans who grew up touched by the depression will never forget this important adage: A penny saved is a penny earned. But they learned the hard way.

Today's mantra is immediate gratification. Chances are, as an American living in today's material world, you haven't been given a lot of encouragement to save your money. In fact, you're encouraged to spend—usually on credit. Couple this live-for-today attitude with a serious lack of financial education, and you have a nation in serious debt—over $1 trillion, not counting mortgages. And debt is usually the antithesis of saving and investing.

Where does that leave you, the would-be personal investor who wants to get into the stock market but has limited funds, annoying debt, and little knowledge of investment vehicles? Probably just making it paycheck to paycheck, with a small savings account languishing somewhere? You might also have a nagging voice in your head that keeps you up at night with the million-dollar question: How will I be able to afford what I want in life, whether it's buying a house, financing education, or retiring comfortably, when most of my money is used for day-to-day living?

That so many of us face anxiety about our finances is the bad news. But here's the good news: You can find a way, on just dollars a day, to create an investing plan that works for you. As we said in the introduction, you won't find a magic, get-rich-quick, money-for-nothing scheme in this book. But you will find the knowledge, sources, and options to build a solid financial future for yourself.

By buying this book, you've proved to yourself that you're willing to learn about investing, and you're willing to set aside money to invest—even if it is only $5 a day. But $5 a day is also approximately $150 a month. And with that amount of money, you can make significant strides toward financial security.

Let's look at the positive aspects of having only $5 a day to invest. Limitations help you prioritize. And prioritizing will help you develop those very qualities that you will need to stick with a solid financial plan, the three traits mentioned earlier—commitment, discipline, and patience.

Your responsibility is cultivating those traits. Ours is to lead you through the basics of investing and to show you how you can enter Wall Street on $5 a day. This means more than taking you on a tour of Wall Street, although that's part of it. Investing is a lifelong process. Once you get started, it's up to you to monitor your investments and to make changes when necessary. This book will take you through the basics of personal finance and the basics of the stock market, and it will give you the resources and information you need to choose and maintain the investments that work for you. You'll also find the phone numbers, names of companies, and sources that will arm you with the information you need to put your knowledge into action.

First, though, you have to have the $5 a day to invest. Otherwise, it's just virtual reality. You also need to set goals. Otherwise, you'll end up choosing investment vehicles that may not be compatible with your time horizon, risk tolerance, and lifestyle.

This is a commonsense guide to Wall Street. And not only can you enter Wall Street on $5 a day but you can actually thrive. It may not be dramatic—at first. You may not become wealthy—at first. But with consistency, knowledge, and foresight, you have the real possibility of building a financial future that is based on solid ground.

Anyone can do it.

WALL STREET WISDOM: ***According to researchers Thomas Stanley and William Danko, typical millionaires earn their fortunes on their own, live well below their means, and invest, rather than spend, their income.***

Almost 37 percent drive used cars, and many have lived in the same house for the last twenty years.

THE POWER OF MONEY

In its most basic sense, investing *is* about using money to make money. Pretty straightforward, right? You put money into an investment and hope to get even more out of it.

Although you don't need a lot of money to make money—we're talking $5 a day, remember?—the more you can put away, the better. The sooner you realize this, the better off your investment life will be. In fact, it's just as important to pay attention to the 95 percent of the money you spend as it is to pay attention to the 5 percent that you invest. When you pay attention to the money that you spend, it will likely mean that you are saving more. When you save money, you can invest it. And investing allows you to earn compound interest, the magic of the stock market.

In fact, when Albert Einstein was asked to name the most powerful force on earth, he reportedly answered, ''Compound interest.'' In simple terms, compound interest is interest on your interest. When you use this simple tool over time, the results can be amazing. However, it's not a quick buck or immediate gratification. But then, what good things in life are? What does compound interest look like to you, the investor with $5 a day?

Compound Interest

Compound interest is a powerful tool for building wealth. The sooner you start investing, the greater the compounding effect will be. In this chart, we're going to take a conservative estimate of return: 8 percent. (Historically, the average return of the stock market is 10 percent.) And we're going to assume that your money is growing tax-deferred, in a 401(k) or IRA account (you'll learn about these in chapter 4).

Even with this conservative approach, by saving just $5 a day at age twenty-five, you will accumulate over $500,000! Even if you get started later, you'll reap benefits. If you start saving at age forty-five instead of twenty-five, you can accumulate nearly $90,000 on $5 a day.

ASSUMPTION: RETIRE AT AGE SIXTY-FIVE

Monthly Savings	$150	$150	$150	$150	$150
Return Rate	8.0%	8.0%	8.0%	8.0%	8.0%
Begin Saving at	25	30	35	40	45
Years to Invest	40	35	30	25	20
Total Invested	$72,000	$63,000	$54,000	$45,000	$36,000
Tax Deferred Savings @ age 65	$523,651.17	$344,082.37	$223,553.92	$142,653.96	$88,353.06

If you start later than age twenty-five and would still like to receive the same savings goal of $523,651.17 at age 65, compounding is still very much in your favor. You just need to increase the amount you save. If we use the age forty-five as an example, you would have to save $29.63 a day instead of $5 a day. (And the title *Wall Street on $29.63* a day is not nearly as catchy.)

	Starting at age 30	Starting at age 35	Starting at age 40	Starting at age 45
Monthly savings	$228.28	$351.36	$550.62	$889.02
Add'l Inv needed to reach $523,651	$95,878	$126,489	$165,185	$213,365

But I Want to Be a Millionaire

What if you want to go for the magical million mark? One very effective way to boost your wealth is to save all or part of any raises or bonuses that you earn, or any cash gifts that you receive. In the following table, if you give your $5 a day a raise of 5 percent per year (we're using the forty-year model here), you can boost your final to over 1 million! Shouldn't be difficult to do. Just think, your first-year raise is only 25 cents per day.

Age	Monthly savings increasing 5% annually	Annual savings	One-year apprecia-tion @ 8%	Accumulated savings
25	$150	$1,800.00	$1,867.49	$1,867.49
26	$158	$1,890.00	$1,960.86	$3,977.75
27	$165	$1,984.50	$2,058.91	$6,354.88
28	$174	$2,083.73	$2,161.85	$9,025.12
29	$182	$2,187.91	$2,269.94	$12,017.07
30	$191	$2,297.31	$2,383.44	$15,361.88
31	$201	$2,412.17	$2,502.61	$19,093.45
32	$211	$2,532.78	$2,627.74	$23,248.67
33	$222	$2,659.42	$2,759.13	$27,867.69
34	$233	$2,792.39	$2,897.09	$32,994.19
35	$244	$2,932.01	$3,041.94	$38,675.67
36	$257	$3,078.61	$3,194.04	$44,963.77

Age	Monthly savings increasing 5% annually	Annual savings	One-year apprecia-tion @ 8%	Accumulated savings
37	$269	$3,232.54	$3,353.74	$51,914.61
38	$283	$3,394.17	$3,521.43	$59,589.21
39	$297	$3,563.88	$3,697.50	$68,053.84
40	$312	$3,742.07	$3,882.38	$77,380.53
41	$327	$3,929.17	$4,076.49	$87,647.46
42	$344	$4,125.63	$4,280.32	$98,939.58
43	$361	$4,331.91	$4,494.33	$111,349.08
44	$379	$4,548.51	$4,719.05	$124,976.06
45	$398	$4,775.94	$4,955.00	$139,929.15
46	$418	$5,014.73	$5,202.75	$156,326.23
47	$439	$5,265.47	$5,462.89	$174,295.22
48	$461	$5,528.74	$5,736.04	$193,974.88
49	$484	$5,805.18	$6,022.84	$215,515.71
50	$508	$6,095.44	$6,323.98	$239,080.94
51	$533	$6,400.21	$6,640.18	$264,847.60
52	$560	$6,720.22	$6,972.19	$293,007.59
53	$588	$7,056.23	$7,320.80	$323,769.00
54	$617	$7,409.04	$7,686.84	$357,357.36
55	$648	$7,779.50	$8,071.18	$394.017.12
56	$681	$8,168.47	$8,474.74	$434,013.23
57	$715	$8,576.89	$8,898.48	$477,632.76
58	$750	$9,005.74	$9,343.40	$525,186.79
59	$788	$9,456.03	$9,810.57	$577,012.30
60	$827	$9,928.83	$10,301.10	$633,474.38
61	$869	$10,425.27	$10,816.15	$694,968.48
62	$912	$10,946.53	$11,356.96	$761,922.92
63	$958	$11,493.86	$11,924.81	$834,801.56
64	$1,006	$12,068.55	$12,521.05	$914,106.73
65	$1,056	$12,671.98	$13,147.10	$1,000,382.37

THE ABCs

Investing involves two components: saving the money you need to invest and finding the right vehicles in which to invest. How do you do this? First, you have to cultivate a Wall Street lifestyle—a lifestyle that includes saving as part of your raison d'etre. Next, you also have to put a name and a financial goal to your investments. Once you know what you are saving for, you can make the best choices for your investments.

There are plenty of ways to save money and we'll talk about these in a minute. Therefore, you can choose the methods that are easiest for you. The idea is to begin to save the money that you are now spending on things you won't even remember a year from now. Instead, you'll want to filter your money into the best investment around—yourself.

Pay Yourself First

Since you are your own best investment, get into the habit of paying yourself first. What this means is that you pay yourself with the same commitment and regularity that you pay your landlord, mortgage company, bank loan officer, or phone company.

WALL STREET WISDOM: ***Only one out of every twenty American families pays themselves first—that is, considers a payment to a savings or investment plan as necessary as a rent or mortgage payment. Coincidentally or not, that's the same number of families—one in twenty—who are financially self-sufficient at retirement.***

WALL STREET WISDOM: ***What happens if you're really in over your head? If you have bills that you can't pay, first take a deep breath. Then tell yourself that this is an opportunity to reorganize your financial life. And then pick up the phone.***

1. **Contact your creditors.** *Let them know that you're aware of the outstanding bill and that you do intend to pay it.*
2. **Set up a payment plan.** *See what kind of payment your creditors can offer you. See what you can afford. Strike an agreement—and then stick with it. Always pay something, rather than missing a payment altogether.*
3. **Start anew.** *This is your opportunity to not only get out of debt, but also to stay out of it. Investing is one way of building up your nest egg so the wolf keeps further away from your door.*

Now, for those who are saying, "I can't afford any more out of my budget right now," and "How will I survive putting money away for the future when I can barely pay my bills now?"

The following will show you how to find the money for investing that you never knew you had.

Trim the Fat

Here are twenty-one ways in which you can painlessly cut expenses. Most professional athletes know the rules: You can break an old habit and cultivate a new one in twenty-one days. And if you can find a way to incorporate one conscious saving ploy every day for twenty-one days, you're on the road to investing.

Keep in mind that like strict food diets, strict budgets can backfire. You may start out motivated and focused, only to lose steam when you feel as though you are denying yourself things that actually make you feel good and alive. The key is to balance saving with living. In other words, the idea is not to deprive yourself to the point where you give up but to enable you to save money where you may be needlessly wasting it.

WALL STREET WISDOM: ***We know of a financial planner who has a special deal for his clients: If he cannot find $100 extra dollars a month in their budget without significantly changing their lifestyle, he offers his services for free.***

1. **Use credit sparingly.** This is a big one. Credit card debt is one of the greatest drains on the American bank account. You wouldn't consider taking out a car loan at 17 percent, and yet that's what many consumers pay for credit card interest rates. With rates these high, it's no wonder that issuers are eager to issue new cards. Remember, credit card issuers are not looking for responsible people; they are looking for people who will make them money. And the best way for a credit card company to make money is for you to carry a balance on your credit card. So don't feel flattered when credit card issuers litter your mailbox with gold card offers—they're just sniffing for business.

   Your best bet is to decide your credit card needs, get the lowest rates you can, and pay your balance every month. Always practice restraint with your credit cards. You certainly don't want to be paying an extra 16.5 percent for a casual dinner out, or 22 percent more for a new winter coat. (Imagine the sale signs for these deals—they would be a lot more honest: BUY NOW AND SPEND FORTY DOLLARS MORE!)

If you are carrying credit card debt of more than 6.9 percent, your single best investment is paying down your debt. Here's a saying that might help put debt in perspective: If you can't pay as you go, you're going too fast.

The average American household credit card debt is $2,100, at an average interest rate of 16.9 percent. With this balance, at this rate, you will end up paying $354.90 per year in interest, or nearly a dollar a day. If you maintain this balance for forty years, you will have paid over $14,000 in interest. If, however, you took that same money and invested it in the stock market, at a conservative 8 percent return, you would earn over $94,000. Enough said.

2. **Prepay your credit card bills.** The reason it feels like you're on a treadmill when you pay only the minimum amount on your credit cards is that most of your payment is going toward interest on the loan. Very little is applied to the principal.

   Always pay off your credit card debt as soon as possible. Consider this: If you pay only the minimum on a $3,000 credit card bill at 17.9 percent interest every month, it will take you sixteen years to pay it off. If you pay only $25 above the minimum each month, it will save you ten years and $2,000 worth of interest payments. You may even consider bimonthly payments. Even by paying the monthly minimum in *two* monthly payments—one every two weeks—you're cutting back on your interest payments. Call your credit card issuer and ask how they want your additional payments. If they charge you a fee, forget it.

You also want to look for the lowest-rate cards available. You can do this through the Bankcard Holders of America at 524 Branch Drive, Salem, Virginia, 24153. For a small fee, they will provide you with their "Debt Zapper," a list of low interest–rate cards. Here are a few more credit card tips: If you do *not* pay off your full balance every month, find the lowest-rate card possible. If you do, carry a no-annual-fee card. Know *how* to shop for the best credit card. In addition to comparing rates and annual fees, compare grace periods, late fees, and cash advance fees. Be especially wary of garnering cash advances through your credit card. The interest rate is usually higher than what you pay for regular purchases, and often there is no grace period.

3. **Prepay your mortgage.** It's the same idea as prepaying your credit card bills. All you need to do is send in more of a monthly payment than you are required to do. Why would you do this? Because you always want to get rid of interest payments as soon as you can! It's amazing, too, what a little extra money paid per day can do. Take a look at the following table. It illustrates what prepayments of one dollar or less a day can save you on your mortgage. For example, if you pay only 25 cents more a day on your mortgage—approximately $7.50 a month—you will save $6,764 off a $25,000, 30-year mortgage at 8 percent.

SAVINGS FROM PREPAYING YOUR MORTGAGE BY PENNIES A DAY (30-YEAR MORTGAGE AT 8 PERCENT)

Prepayment amount per day	Savings on a $25,000 mortgage	Savings on a $50,000 mortgage	Savings on a $75,000 mortgage	Savings on a $100,000 mortgage	Savings on a $125,000 mortgage
10 cents	$3,079	$3,234	$3,289	$3,317	$3,334
25 cents	$6,764	$7,527	$7,826	$7,986	$8,084
50 cents	$11,324	$13,534	$14,506	$15,054	$15,406
$1.00	$17,268	$22,657	$25,400	$27,072	$28,200

Source: *The Banker's Secret Bulletin.* Good Advice Press (800–255–0899).

4. **Stop paying your private mortgage insurance as soon as you can.** If you own a home and are still paying your private mortgage insurance (PMI), stop as soon as you build up 20 percent equity in your home. PMI is credit insurance that helps out the lender; it offers insurance in case you default on your mortage. *You* don't lose out when it stops. Rates are typically one-third to two-thirds of one percent on a 30-year mortgage. PMI remains a part of your annual payments for the entire loan—or until you have it removed.

   While lenders love PMI and are loathe to drop it, they usually will after you've built up 20 percent equity in your home. You'll need to get an appraisal that proves that your current loan-to-value is approximately 75 to 80 percent. A tip, though: Call your lender and ask for an approved appraiser.
5. **Reduce your property taxes.** Since property taxes are

an imprecise tax determined by the subjective appraisal of an assessor, many homeowners are overpaying. In fact, most Americans don't even think to check to see if they are paying a fair property tax rate.

In most states, the records are accessible to the public, usually in the public library. Look up the records for homes near yours that are of similar size—and have similar features. If you think you're being overtaxed, file a challenge with the local assessor's office, and ask for a property tax abatement. Be prepared to stick to your guns. You may be able to save several hundred dollars per year.

6. **Shop for the best long-distance phone carrier.** Nearly half of all Americans are paying standard phone rates—that means the highest rates possible—for their long-distance telephone service. Part of this is due to ignorance. Most consumers are not even aware of their choices. The deregulation of the phone industry in the early 1980s created a boom in long-distance phone companies: several *hundred* long-distance carriers now exist. And many of the smaller, newer companies offer comparable service to the well-known, larger ones. Shop around for the cheapest rate.

   In fact, you have to shop around, because here's the kicker: You are not automatically apprised of the newest, lowest rates from your current carrier. Unless you initiate a call to your long-distance carrier, or one of the long-distance companies happens to catch you at home during a subscriber campaign, you won't even know about the latest, lowest rates. Therefore, ask. And keep asking since rates change constantly. Find out what they can offer you. You can save, depending on your long-distance telephone usage, up to $100 a month.

One good way to do your research is to contact the Telecommunication Research & Action Center (TRAC), a nonprofit watchdog group based in Washington, D.C., at P.O. Box 27279, Washington, D.C. 20005. Or contact Teleworth, the Internet telecommunications company at www.teleworth.com. On this Web site, you can determine the best long-distance phone company based on your calling patterns. You can even switch long-distance carriers on-line.

Also, use the free 800 directory assistance number (800–555–1212) to see if a company has a toll-free number before dialing long distance. It's another painless way to save.

7. **Eat out one meal less a month.** Just one less meal out a month can save you anywhere from $8 to $40. Pick the meal that you really don't enjoy—you know the one—the meal that you're grabbing on the fly because you're late, stressed out, or bored. Consider your meals out a treat for special occasions or for food that you can't get at home; otherwise, you're just paying 40 percent more for scrambled eggs.
8. **Don't overinsure yourself.** Although insurance is necessary, you may be paying for coverage you don't need—or you may be paying rates that are too high. Your first order of business is to shop around. Do you have the most cost-effective life, health, disability, and homeowner's insurance? Often insurance companies offer a discount if you buy more than one type of insurance from them, or if you have a low-risk lifestyle.

   Also, look at your deductibles—they may be too high. For example, if your car is more than six years old, consider raising the deductible or switching to liability only. Also, are you buying life insurance but have no dependents? Consider forego your policy and use that same money for your own investments instead (you'll find more about life insurance in chapter 2).

WALL STREET WISDOM: ***Do you know what's what on your paycheck stub? See if you can answer the following questions (no fair looking):***

How much are you paying for health coverage? How much is taken out for taxes? How much is your gross pay? (That's what you earn.) How much is your net pay? (That's what you take home.) You're a step ahead if you know how to read your paycheck. Here's a brief anatomy of a paycheck stub.

Federal income tax: *This amount goes straight to the IRS. How does your employer know how much to withhold? It depends on your marital status, how often you get paid, and the number of withholding allowances that you claim on your W-4 Form—the form you fill out when you are hired.*

A word of caution: Reconsider if you purposefully claim the highest level of dependents you can in order to receive a larger refund from the IRS. Instead, consider collecting this money as take-home pay and using it as part of your $5 a day stash. Otherwise, it's as if you're giving the IRS an interest-free loan.

In addition to the federal income tax, most states and towns tax you as well.

Federal Insurance Contributions Act (FICA): *This amount goes to Social Security and Medicare. Here's how it works: American workers subsidize American retirees through their Social Security contributions. However, the population is aging. Therefore, by the time the baby boomers reach maturity, there will be only one American working for every three retirees, the inverse of what it is today.*

Your employer matches your contribution to both Social Security and Medicare. If you're self-employed, you pay both halves.

State Disability Insurance Tax (SDI): *This applies only to residents of California, Hawaii, New Jersey, New York, Rhode Island and Puerto Rico. This tax provides residents of these states with benefits if they are disabled by a non-work event or illness.*

Pretax retirement plans, such as 401(k) or 4013(b): *These plans are entirely voluntary, and the amounts withheld depend on whether you've chosen to enroll in these plans, and how much you've chosen to contribute. As you'll find out in chapter 4, these investments come out of your paycheck before taxes. In other words, they are tax-deductible.*

Health care benefits: *Health care benefits are one of the most desired company benefits. Your employer typically subsidizes your involvement in a health plan, and often includes life insurance as well. Your part of the payment comes out of your paycheck before taxes. Some employers also allow pretax accounts for child care.*

9. **Take care of your car.** Not only will your car thank you but you'll also have money to show for it. A well-tuned car saves you approximately 10 percent in gas bills. Any extra weight you're carrying around—in your car, of course—costs you, too. Your car loses about a half mile on the gallon for every 100 pounds it carries. So clean out your trunk, change your oil, and get regular tune-ups. And always remember to wear your seat belt.
10. **Watch your food bills.** A University of Florida researcher found that most grocery store shoppers could not name the cost of an item seconds after putting it into their cart. If you do this kind of grocery shopping, you're wasting money that could be invested in the stock market.

    Start by planning out your meals first. And then when you do go to shop, carry a set amount of cash instead of your checkbook or credit card so you're not tempted to splurge. By doing these two things—

shopping prepared and avoiding the temptation of unlimited payment means—you can easily cut back on your weekly food bill by 10 percent. And, of course, never shop hungry. Even if you have your menu planned and only $40 dollars in your pocket, you could end up with $35 worth of whatever you lay eyes on first.

11. **Bring your lunch to work.** This is easy. Stock up on the foods you like, and brown-bag it. Lunches out can be a major financial drain—to the tune of $35 a week if you eat out every day. Watch what happens when you cut back. You might find it addictive. Chances are, you'll end up eating healthier, too.
12. **Kick the habit.** Do you really need another reason to stop smoking? OK, here it is: A pack-a-day smoker spends at least $750 a year on his habit.
13. **Shop discount.** Really, it matters. You can get the same merchandise for one-third to one-half off at the discount stores that you'll find at brand-name department stores. The stores are often not as well-organized, the merchandise is not as well-packaged, and you sometimes have to fight for your size. But you can save significant amounts of money—and not deprive yourself at all. You might want to get in the habit of looking for a 10 percent savings on anything that you buy. Ten percent is the historic return on the stock market—and a great investment return.
14. **Shop at the right time of year.** Although it's hard to consider winter coats when you've just shed yours in April, you might find a coat for $40 instead of the $180 you would spend in November. Many consumer goods are tied to seasons. Your job is to search for them when they're out of season. Air conditioners are cheaper in winter; holiday gizmos, right after the holi-

day. Plan ahead and have some patience, and you'll save money.

15. **Cut medical bills.** If you need a prescription, ask your doctor for free samples. Ask for an itemized bill if you're hospitalized, and then check for accuracy. Save emergency room visits for real emergencies. And take good care of yourself. Take your vitamins, exercise, eat right, and do things that you enjoy. Prevention is nine-tenths of the cure.
16. **Negotiate.** This means everything from car price—whether you're buying or leasing—to hotel room rates to your doctor's fees. Nearly everything in life is negotiable. You just have to ask.
17. **Pay your bills on time.** Those late fees really add up, to say nothing of putting your credit at risk. One of the easiest ways to pay on time is through automatic payment plans. You simply give your gas or utility company a canceled check and fill out a form, and they will deduct the amount you owe each month. Not only will you save on late fees but you'll also save money on stamps, envelopes, and checks. Don't forget

WALL STREET WISDOM: ***Another way to take advantage of direct deposit***

Instead of taking your IRS refund and spending it on something you won't even remember in a few months, add it to your $5-a-day fund.

By completing a few extra lines on your tax return that provides the IRS with the routing number to your checking or savings account, you can have your refund deposited directly. Direct deposit also helps to ensure that you actually receive your refund.

In 1996, more than $6 million of refunds were returned to the IRS as undeliverable. Ouch.

to check your billing statements, though—mistakes happen.

18. **Shop around for the best bank.** Banks are feeling the squeeze from brokerage companies, credit unions, and on-line banking services. In turn, they are squeezing you, the consumer, with lots of fees and charges—often hidden. Those innocent little points and penalties on your savings and checking accounts can add up to hundreds of dollars a year. Again, be a conscious shopper. Look for no-fee accounts, reasonable overdraft fees, and realistic minimums.
19. **Buy in bulk.** Unexciting but true. You can save big bucks by piling up.
20. **Do year-round holiday shopping.** Start saving for the holidays at the beginning of the year. Each month contribute a set amount, and make sure that you have boundaries on what you plan on spending. That way, you're prepared for the rush, you won't be as tempted to overspend, and it will reduce your holiday stress level.
21. **Ignore the Joneses.** John Kenneth Galbraith said that the present American economic structure is based not only on the satisfaction of desire but also on the creation of desire. Keep that in mind. If you can't afford to pay cash for something—you can't afford to buy it.

***WALL STREET WISDOM:** If the road to investing—or even saving—is hindered by over-your-head debt, you may want to consider counseling:*

1. ***Consumer Credit Counseling Service (National Foundation for Consumer Credit):** 8611 Second Avenue, Suite 100, Silver Spring, MD 20910; 301-589-5600. Provides free or low-cost financial counseling. To locate the CCCS office closest to you, call 800-338-2227.*
2. ***Consumer Fresh Start:** 601 Pennsylvania Avenue NW, Suite 900, Washington, D.C. 20004; 800-933-2372.*
3. ***Debtors Anonymous:** Modeled after the 12-step program of Alcoholics Anonymous, the national headquarters is located at P.O. Box 400, Grand Central Station, New York, New York 10163–0400.*

ESTABLISHING YOUR GOALS

You now know how to put your money to its best use, whether it's for pleasure or necessity. Now it's time to take the next steps in investing: Figuring out your cash flow and establishing your goals. It may sound obvious, but you need to know how much money you have to invest. (Of course, we want you to find at least $5 a day.) And you need to discern your financial goals—what you want money for.

Establishing your financial goals gives you a road map to investing. Once you know what you're saving for—and how much money you will need for those goals—you can choose the best investments for you. This way you're not risking early withdrawal penalties, vulnerability to market volatility, and rash investment decisions.

TRACKING YOUR INCOME AND EXPENSES

At the end of chapters 1, 2, 4, and 5, you'll find a special section called Ask a Financial Planner. In this section, a professional financial planner, Darryl Reed of the national fee-only investment firm, Money Minds, "confers"—with six fictional clients. We've created these clients to reflect common real-life situations. Reed will lead these clients—Joe, Tess and David, Carla, and John and Marge—through the beginning stages of investing to creating a portfolio. It's a way for you, the reader, to create your own financial plan. The first step is to track where your money is going. How do you do that? On page (34), you'll find a Financial Management Worksheet, the very same one that Darryl Reed uses with his real-life clients. This worksheet allows you to track how much money comes into your household, how much goes out, and where you can make room for more. Take a few minutes now to fill out this form. It requires you to list your income, expenses, and debt payments. How much excess cash are you left with each month? If it's not enough to give you $5 a day for investing, where can you cut back? Refer back to this chapter to see where you can find the money that you need.

TIME LINE

Next, you need to spell out some financial goals. One of the simplest ways to discern your life—and financial—goals is by creating a time line. A time line is simply a way of writing down your goals and assigning a dollar amount to each.

First, divide your financial goals into three categories: short-term, mid-term, and long-term. Short-term goals are anything you want to do or buy within the next three years; mid-term goals are ones you'd like to achieve within the next three to five years; and long-term goals are anything you are planning to do five years down the road or later.

What are some common goals? Buying a house, buying a new car, a vacation, college education for yourself or your children, a vacation home. And don't forget retirement. Then simply draw a line, representing a certain period of time. Then note your goals at the appropriate time intervals. How much will you need for each goal? Jot that down as well.

---

0 1 2 3 4 5 YEARS 6 7 8 9 10 YEARS

When you combine your time line with the Financial Management Worksheet, you'll have a good idea of how much money you'll need to accomplish your goals. This will help you determine what types of investments you will choose. Of course, you may realize that what you desire isn't quite in line with your current financial situation. You may have to start small, make more lifestyle changes, and change your goals slightly. One thing is for sure, though—taking a look at your finances and goals will help you realize how important it is to just get started.

Ultimately, investing is about using your money to work for you. And when you know where you're going and you take action to get you started on the path, it's quite likely that you'll end up there.

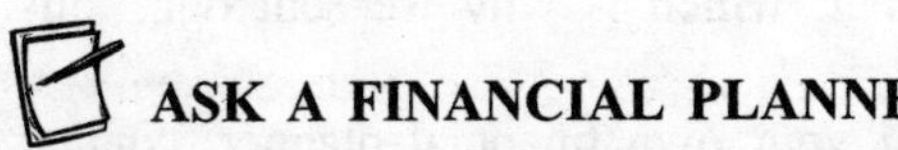

ASK A FINANCIAL PLANNER

In this section, we're going to follow the progress of fictional planning clients—two individuals and two couples: Joe;

Carla; Tess and David; and Marge and John. These clients are in different stages of life. We asked a fee-only financial planner based in Alabama, to review their situations. Darryl Reed, of Money Minds.

Financial planners make a living helping others manage their finances. Unlike a stockbroker, a financial planner will get involved in all of your finances, including stocks, bonds, insurance, tax planning, and even real estate. Together, you will discuss your goals and find a way to meet them. Hundreds of thousands of people call themselves financial planners, partly because this profession is not licensed by the government. However, there are some ways to choose the best one for you, if you decide that you need the assistance. First of all, know the types. A *fee-only* planner will charge you either an annual fee or an hourly fee. Fee-only planners give advice, but they do not sell products. Therefore, you do not have to deal with a conflict of interest.

Commission-only planners do not charge a fee, but they receive a commission on the investment products that they sell. However, you can benefit from one-stop shopping. Remember, though, a commission-only planner may have a vested interest in selling you a certain product. In other words, there may be a conflict of interest.

Fee plus commission planners may charge you a fee for their overall financial planning, but they may also charge you a commission on the products that they sell. However, the commission may be lower than it would be with a commission-only planner. Obviously, there are advantages to using a fee-only financial planner, which is why we sent our "clients" to one.

If you're looking for your own financial planner, contact one of the following associations for a list of members in your area:

Institute of Certified Financial Planners
3801 E. Florida Avenue
Suite 708
Denver, CO 80210
303-759-4900

International Association for Financial Planning
2 Concourse Parkway, Suite 800
Atlanta, GA 30328
404-395-1605

National Association of Personal Financial Advisors (NAPFA)
1130 Lake Cook Road
Buffalo Grove, Illinois 60089
800-366-2732

Reed's first step was to use the Financial Management Worksheet to get a sense of the clients' income, expenses, investments, and debt before he began their investment strategy. Then he sat down with them to see where they could cut back. Together, they formulated a savings and investing plan. We'll visit with Joe, Carla, Tess, David, Marge, and John as they go about creating their investment portfolios.

For this first chapter, we'll look at their cash flow analyses. We'll see how they're going to budget so that they can invest $5 a day. But first let's meet the clients.

- *Joe Lucas,* 26, is a reporter for a suburban Boston newspaper. He took this job two years ago, when he left graduate school. His monthly take-home pay is $1,800. He has access to a 401(k) plan at work, with matching contributions. He also has access to health, life, and disability insurance. He is driving a nine-year-old Honda right now, with no car payments. He shares an apartment with two roommates, which keeps his rent down, but he pays a lot for his urban social life. He has $400 in a low-interest savings account.

• *Tess and David Shields,* both 35, have one child, Sonny, 3. David is a teacher, with a monthly take-home paycheck of $2,300. Tess is also a teacher, but she has worked part-time since having Sonny. Her monthly take-home paycheck is $1,200. They pay approximately $1,200 per month for housing, including mortgage payment, taxes, and utilities. Child care payments cost approximately $350 per month. David has access to a 403(b) plan at his job, where he has been working for the past five years, but he hasn't contributed anything yet. They have $3,000 in a NOW account. They get health and disability insurance through David's work. They have no life insurance.

• *Carla Smith,* age 47, is a single mom, with two children, ages 9 and 10. She works as an administrative assistant at a small landscaping firm. Her take-home pay is $2,600 per month. Her monthly housing costs are approximately $900 per month, including rent and utilities. Her car payment is $225 per month. She has a pension plan at work, but no 401(k). She has health insurance through work, but no life or disability insurance. Her credit card debt is $2,000 at 17.5 percent. She has no savings accounts or investments.

• *Marge and John Le Boucher,* age 65. John recently retired as a salesman for Hart's Brewery. While John worked, Marge stayed at home and raised their three children. John had a defined pension plan, which now pays him $1,400 per month. He also receives $470 per month from Social Security. They own their home, but taxes are $4,000 per year. They helped put their kids through college, so they have only $4,000 in a money market account. Neither is adverse to working part-time.

GETTING STARTED: FILLING OUT THE FINANCIAL MANAGEMENT WORKSHEET, AND CREATING A TIME LINE

• **Darryl Reed speaks:** Joe's original Financial Management Worksheet showed a plus margin of only $20. Since his time line shows goals of a new car and a home within seven years or so, this wasn't going to work. I suggested that he cut back on his phone usage, gifts, cable TV, and personal grooming. I also suggested that he be more careful tracking where his ''miscellaneous'' cash was going—a common money pit. He was able to free up an additional $180 per month. We were free to begin an investment plan.

• On their time line, Tess and David placed buying a new car, college funding for their child, retirement planning, and a trip to Disneyland. Tess and David needed a lot of assistance in cutting back in order to free up money. They cut back from two phone lines to one; shopped around for more affordable home and auto insurance (they were able to get a discount by buying from the same company); they cut back on their entertainment; and they cut back on gift buying. They also realized that they were not making use of David's prescription drug card, which was part of his health insurance plan from work. In addition, by cutting their miscellaneous spending they were able to free up $195 per month.

• Carla's goals included getting out of debt, buying a house, and retirement and college planning. She needed a lot of help. I had her cut back on dry cleaning, entertainment, personal care, and miscellaneous. Other things I wanted her to look at were ways of generating addi-

WALL STREET REVISITED: Checklist for chapter 1

1. *Decide that you are ready and willing to enter Wall Street. Investing stems from saving. And saving requires commitment and discipline.*
2. *Debt is one of the premiere reasons why Americans have trouble getting ahead in their financial life. Take a look at your credit habits. Are you paying interest on credit cards with money that can be used for your $5-a-day investment plan?*
3. *You can probably trim at least $100 a month from your spending by just being aware of where your unnecessary expenses are. Don't be afraid to look at your lifestyle carefully, and make adjustments. You just need to strike the appropriate attitude. This isn't about sacrifice; it's about discipline.*
4. *Fill out a Fiancial Management Worksheet. See what your financial obligations are, and how much money you have to work with.*
5. *Create a time line of financial goals. If you don't list specific goals, such as a car, house, or new CD player, with accompanying specific dollar amounts, you'll be tempted to not follow through. You need to know how much money you're aiming for—and why—to create the most effective investment portfolio.*
6. *If you can't find at least $5 a day to invest, go back to your cash analysis sheet and see where you can cut back. The idea is to get your money working for you, in a way that serves you best.*

tional income and transferring her debt to a lower interest–rate card. Part-time work is almost always a viable option for those who need more cash. And you always want to pay as little interest as possible.

• Marge and John have simple goals: travel, increased financial security, and home improvements. I had them cut back on their personal care and miscellaneous expenses to reach a surplus monthly amount of $150. I also suggested that they consider outside part-time employment, since they made it clear that they would be open to this.

FINANCIAL MANAGEMENT WORKSHEET

Source of *Monthly* Income

Wage Earnings (After Tax)	$______
Other's Earnings	______
Support/Alimony/Etc.	______
Other Income	______
Total	$______ (1)

Current *Monthly* Savings/Investments

Savings	$______
401K/Stock Purchase/Etc.	______
Total	$______ (2)

Basic *Monthly* Expenses

Mortgage/Rent	$______
Property Tax	______
Heat/Fuel	______
Electricity	______
House & Lawn Maintenance	______
Telephone	______
Long Distance	______
Water/Sewage	______
Garbage	______
Groceries	______
Meals Out	______

Outstanding Consumer Debt

Debt/Loan	*Outstanding Balance*	*Monthly Payments*
Equity Credit Line	______	______
401K Loans	______	______
Recreational Vehicle(s)	______	______
Credit Cards	______	______
______	______	______
______	______	______
______	______	______
______	______	______

Child Care ________
Child Support ________
Auto Payment ________
Gasoline ________
Car Maintenance ________
Bus or Car Pool ________
Insurance:
Auto ________
Home Owner's/Renters ________
Medical ________
Life ________
Laundry/Dry Cleaning ________
Clothing ________
Entertainment ________
Vacation ________
Other Expenses:
Cigarettes ________
Alcohol ________
Prescription Drugs ________
Gifts ________
Religious/Charities ________
Cable T.V. ________
Dues & Subscriptions ________
Personal Care ________
Misc. ________

Total Expenses **$________ (3)**

________	________	________
________	________	________
________	________	________
________	________	________
________	________	________
________	________	________
________	________	________
________	________	________
Other Debt	________	________
________	________	________
________	________	________
________	________	________
Total Debt	**$________**	________ **(4)**

Cash Management Plan Summary (Monthly)

Total Income	$________ (1)
(Less) Savings/Investments	- (________) (2)
(Less) Basic Expenses	- (________) (3)
(Less) Debt Payments	- (________) (4)
Margin	**$________**

NAME: JOE LUCAS
FINANCIAL MANAGEMENT WORKSHEET

Source of *Monthly* Income

Wage Earnings (After Tax)	$ 1800
Other's Earnings	
Support/Alimony/Etc.	
Other Income	
Total	**$** 1800 **(1)**

Current *Monthly* Savings/Investments

Savings	$ —
401K/Stock Purchase/Etc.	—
Total	**$** — **(2)**

Basic *Monthly* Expenses

Mortgage/Rent	$ 350
Property Tax	—
Heat/Fuel	—
Electricity	20
House & Lawn Maintenance	—
Telephone	—
Long Distance	-40 80/40
Water/Sewage	—
Garbage	—
Groceries	200
Meals Out	280

Outstanding Consumer Debt

Debt/Loan	*Outstanding Balance*	*Monthly Payments*
Equity Credit Line		
401K Loans		
Recreational Vehicle(s)		
Credit Cards		

Child Care	—
Child Support	—
Auto Payment	—
Gasoline	60
Car Maintenance	60
Bus or Car Pool	—
Insurance:	
Auto	70
Home Owner's/Renters	—
Medical	—
Life	—
Laundry/Dry Cleaning	30
Clothing	50
Entertainment	100
Vacation	40
Other Expenses:	
Cigarettes	—
Alcohol	—
Prescription Drugs	—
Gifts	-30 60/30
Religious/Charities	—
Cable T.V.	-30 60/30
Dues & Subscriptions	—
Personal Care	-20 40/20
Misc.	-40 80/40
Total Expenses	$ 1580 (3)

Other Debt		
School Loan	20,000	200
Total Debt	$	(4)

Cash Management Plan Summary (Monthly)

		After Changes
Total Income	$ 1800 (1)	1800
(Less) Savings/Investments	- (—) (2)	—
(Less) Basic Expenses	- (1580) (3)	1420
(Less) Debt Payments	- (200) (4)	200
Margin	$ 20.00	180

NAME: TESS and DAVID SHIELDS
FINANCIAL MANAGEMENT WORKSHEET

Source of *Monthly* Income

Wage Earnings (After Tax)	$ 3500
Other's Earnings	
Support/Alimony/Etc.	
Other Income	
Total	$ 3500 (1)

Current *Monthly* Savings/Investments

Savings	$
401K/Stock Purchase/Etc.	—
Total	$ — (2)

Basic *Monthly* Expenses

Mortgage/Rent	$ 900
Property Tax	50
Heat/Fuel	60
Electricity	40
House & Lawn Maintenance	60
Telephone	80
Long Distance	-20 80/60
Water/Sewage	40
Garbage	—
Groceries	240
Meals Out	100

Outstanding Consumer Debt

Debt/Loan	*Outstanding Balance*	*Monthly Payments*
Equity Credit Line		
401K Loans		
Recreational Vehicle(s)		
Credit Cards		

Item	Change	Amount
Child Care		350
Child Support		—
Auto Payment		300
Gasoline		60
Car Maintenance		80
Bus or Car Pool		—
Insurance:		
Auto	-10	150/140
Home Owner's/Renters	-20	80/60
Medical		—
Life		—
Laundry/Dry Cleaning		40
Clothing		100
Entertainment	-50	150/100
Vacation		—
Other Expenses:		
Cigarettes		—
Alcohol		—
Prescription Drugs	-30	40/10
Gifts	-20	100/80
Religious/Charities		—
Cable T.V.		—
Dues & Subscriptions		40
Personal Care	-75	150/75
Misc.	-50	100/50
Total Expenses		$ 3590 **(3)**

Other Debt		
Total Debt	$	(4)

Cash Management Plan Summary (Monthly)

			After Changes
Total Income	$ 3500	(1)	3500
(Less) Savings/Investments	- ( )	(2)	
(Less) Basic Expenses	- (3590)	(3)	3315
(Less) Debt Payments	- ( )	(4)	
Margin	$ -90		185

NAME: CARLA SMITH
FINANCIAL MANAGEMENT WORKSHEET

Source of *Monthly* Income

Wage Earnings (After Tax)	$ 2600
Other's Earnings (Selling Avon)	300
Support/Alimony/Etc.	
Other Income	
Total	$ 2600 (1)

Current *Monthly* Savings/Investments

Savings	$
401K/Stock Purchase/Etc.	
Total	$ (2)

Basic *Monthly* Expenses

Mortgage/Rent	$ 750
Property Tax	—
Heat/Fuel	15
Electricity	30
House & Lawn Maintenance	—
Telephone	40
Long Distance	60
Water/Sewage	—
Garbage	—
Groceries	240
Meals Out	180

Outstanding Consumer Debt

Debt/Loan	*Outstanding Balance*	*Monthly Payments*
Equity Credit Line		
401K Loans		
Recreational Vehicle(s)		
Credit Cards	2000	40

Expense	Change	Amount
Child Care		200
Child Support		—
Auto Payment		225
Gasoline		40
Car Maintenance		70
Bus or Car Pool		40
Insurance:		
Auto		80
Home Owner's/Renters		—
Medical		—
Life		—
Laundry/Dry Cleaning	-40	80/40
Clothing		80
Entertainment	-50	180/130
Vacation		—
Other Expenses:		
Cigarettes		40
Alcohol		30
Prescription Drugs		40
Gifts		140
Religious/Charities		—
Cable T.V.		—
Dues & Subscriptions		—
Personal Care	-100	200/100
Misc.	-60	100/40
Total Expenses		$ 2860 **(3)**

Other Debt		
Total Debt	$ 200	40 **(4)**

Cash Management Plan Summary (Monthly)

		After Changes
Total Income	$ 2600 (1)	2900
(Less) Savings/Investments	- ( ) (2)	—
(Less) Basic Expenses	- (2860) (3)	2610
(Less) Debt Payments	- (40) (4)	40
Margin	$ -300	250

NAME: MARGE and JOHN LeBOUCHER
FINANCIAL MANAGEMENT WORKSHEET

Source of *Monthly* Income

Wage Earnings (After Tax)	$+30 1840/1870
Other's Earnings	
Support/Alimony/Etc.	
Other Income	
Total	**$ 1840 (1)**
	New Total 1870

Current *Monthly* Savings/Investments

Savings	$ —
401K/Stock Purchase/Etc.	—
Total	**$ — (2)**

Basic *Monthly* Expenses

Mortgage/Rent	$ —
Property Tax	360
Heat/Fuel	60
Electricity	60
House & Lawn Maintenance	80
Telephone	40
Long Distance	40
Water/Sewage	30
Garbage	30
Groceries	140
Meals Out	60

Outstanding Consumer Debt

Debt/Loan	*Outstanding Balance*	*Monthly Payments*
Equity Credit Line	—	
401K Loans	—	
Recreational Vehicle(s)	—	
Credit Cards	—	

Expense	Adjustment	Amount
Child Care		—
Child Support		—
Auto Payment		170
Gasoline		40
Car Maintenance		50
Bus or Car Pool		—
Insurance:		
Auto		80
Home Owner's/Renters		80
Medical		—
Life		—
Laundry/Dry Cleaning		—
Clothing		40
Entertainment		50
Vacation		50
Other Expenses:		
Cigarettes		—
Alcohol		—
Prescription Drugs		50
Gifts		40
Religious/Charities		40
Cable T.V.		—
Dues & Subscriptions		40
Personal Care	-40	80/40
Misc.	-50	100/50
Total Expenses		$ 1810 **(3)**

Other Debt		
School Loan	20,000	200
Total Debt	$ —	— **(4)**

Cash Management Plan Summary (Monthly)		*After Changes*
Total Income	$ 1840 (1)	1870
(Less) Savings/Investments	- (—) (2)	
(Less) Basic Expenses	- (1810) (3)	1720
(Less) Debt Payments	- ( ) (4)	
Margin	$ 30	150

TWO

Laying the Groundwork for Good Investing

Money won't buy happiness, but it will pay the salaries of a large research staff to study the problem.
—Bill Vaughan

WALL STREET NAVIGATOR: Finding your way around chapter 2

Your first steps toward investing
The importance of opening an accessible savings account
How to choose the right savings account for you
How to protect your assets through insurance
How much insurance to buy, and where to buy it

OK, so you've trimmed the fat from your budget and set your financial goals. Now you have to lay the groundwork for investing. How do you do that? The first step is to protect yourself not from risk, which is inherent in investing, but from *needless* risk.

Risk comes in many forms. Most of us associate investment risk with losing money, period. What happens if I invest in stock A, and it plummets? What happens if I put my money in mutual fund B, and the portfolio manager buys shares in South American cotton shirts, right before Italian ones become all the rage? What happens if my corporate bond isn't repaid? You get the picture. We're afraid to put our money into something—and not get it back.

Just as we can do things that harm us, we can also harm ourselves by *not* doing things. It's not checking the gas tank before that long trip, not training properly before running that 10k, or not getting to bed at a decent hour before that huge presentation that can endanger our well-being, just as much as drinking and driving, eating a high cholesterol diet, or arriving late for work four days a week.

You need to address one of the most basic risks of investing *before* you invest: You need to protect your assets from the unexpected. The best-laid plans of the individual investor can be derailed by a huge medical bill, the need for a new roof, or a car that's stolen with two years of loan payments remaining.

In other words, before you invest, you need to set up a secure and accessible savings account, and you need to protect yourself with health, life, and disability insurance. The greatest hindrance to your investing is interruption. Not only do you risk having to withdraw your money at the worst possible time—think of the stock market crash of 1987, for example—but you also lose out on all that powerful compound interest that we talked about in the first chapter.

Insurance is another important way to reduce your risk. Even though buying insurance is about as much fun as visiting the dentist—and you don't even get the free toothbrush—it's a reality of life. Without it, you risk losing all your money—or being in debt the rest of your life—due to a medical emergency or natural disaster. Think of protecting your assets as placing the first coat of primer on the wall before you paint, preparing the soil before you plant, or warming up before you run.

SAVINGS FIRST

Let's start with your savings account. Experts recommend that you accumulate at least three months' living expenses in an accessible, low-risk savings account before you do anything else with your money. And that's a conservative estimate. Some feel that having less than six months' living expenses in an accessible account is playing Russian roulette with your finances.

Let's be realistic. Your goal is to invest your $5 a day as soon as possible, and it may take you years to accumulate three to six months' living expenses. For example, if your monthly living expenses are $3,000, you're looking at a minimum of $9,000. What you may want to consider instead is whether or not you have other sources of possible income if anything does happen to you. Also, how stable is your job? Your partner's job? Do you have a line of credit in an emergency? If you work in an uncertain industry, or are self-employed, you may want to have more rather than less in your emergency fund. If you have excess cash every month, have no dependents, and are in a very stable career, you may be able to get by with less. It's a personal decision, and completely about your peace of mind. Your goal is to cover yourself in case of an emergency.

You may consider saving a base amount—say, $2,000—in an accessible savings account, and begin to invest your $5 a day while building up your savings account at the same time, although this is riskier than providing yourself with three to six months' living expenses. At no time should you stop saving—or neglect to have your emergency fund.

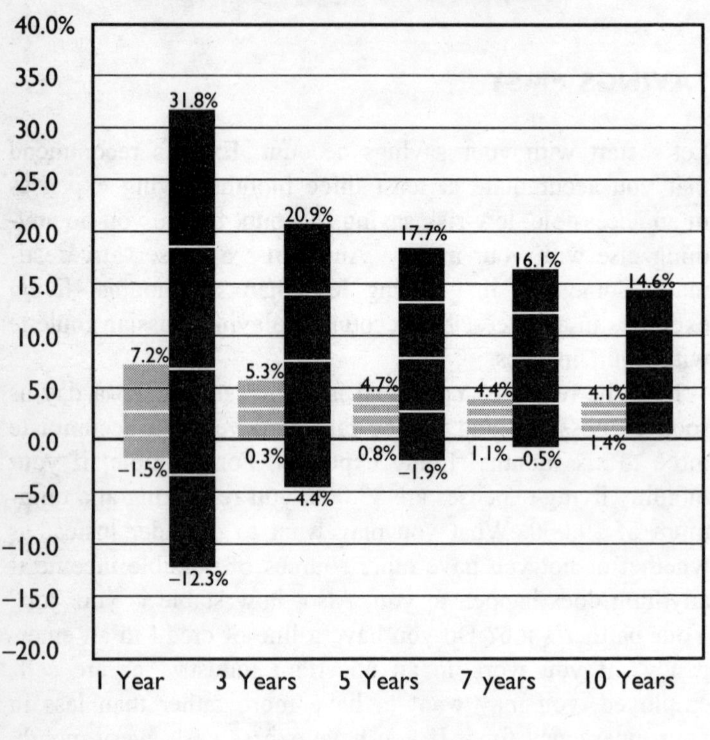

The projected range of average annual returns for your Present and Proposed Composite Asset Mixes are shown over the projection period. The entire range of returns from the best-case to the worst-case outcomes are represented by the bars. There is a 98% chance of realizing a return which is greater than the worst-case return. And, there is a 2% chance of exceeding the best-case return. The range of average returns narrows over longer time periods and for more conservative asset mixes.

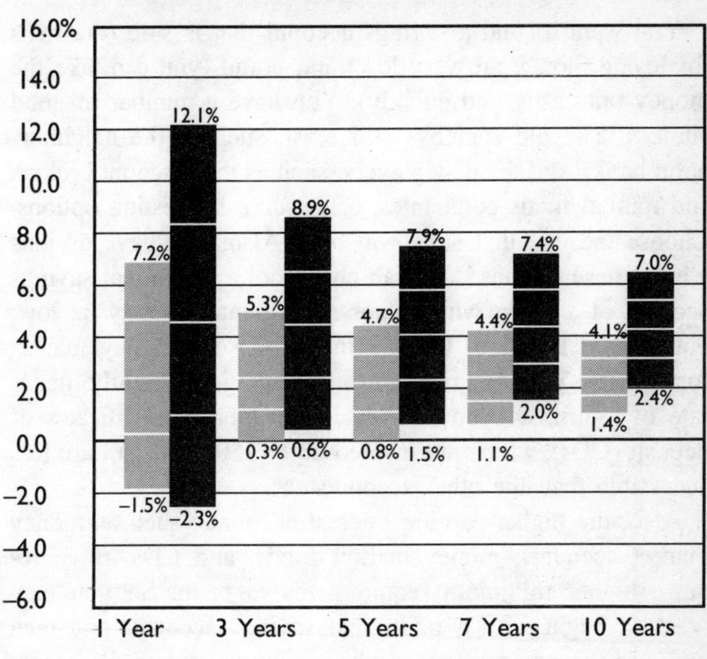

The projected range of average annual returns for your Present and Proposed Composite Asset Mixes are shown over the projection period. The entire range of returns from the best-case to the worst-case outcomes are represented by the bars. There is a 98% chance of realizing a return which is greater than the worst-case return. And, there is a 2% chance of exceeding the best-case return. The range of average returns narrows over longer time periods and for more conservative asset mixes.

The Savings Vehicles

You want to find a savings account that is safe (the risks for losing money are very low) and liquid (you can take the money out easily and quickly). You have a number of good choices. The old standbys still exist, such as the neighborhood bank. And the new players, such as the discount brokers and mutual funds companies, offer some interesting options. Choose the one that suits you best. Also, you have options within these options. You can check out a traditional savings account at a bank, where your rate of interest may be low, but your risk is too. Or you may choose a money market fund, where you may risk a bit more and get a slightly higher rate of return. Or you may decide to look at certificates of deposit (CDs), which are insured up to $100,000, but are less accessible than the other accounts.

Also, the higher-earning interest accounts, such as money market accounts, money market funds, and CDs, often require higher minimum requirements to open. So you may want to begin with a traditional savings account, and then move to the other accounts when you accumulate the necessary amount. Let's take a look at each of these, so that you can make the best decision for you.

Bank Savings Accounts: Traditional bank savings accounts are designed purely for saving money. You can withdraw money from these accounts or move your money to another account within the bank or credit union, but you cannot write a check against these accounts.

Deposits are banks' main source of loan money; therefore, they pay you interest on your savings deposits. This is to entice you to open an account. In addition to checking out the interest rate when you're shopping around for a savings account, you always want to check when your interest is compounded. The more often, the better. Even so, bank savings accounts' interest rates are often low. And as banks struggle to stay competitive in an ever-expanding field, they may use *fees* to keep their bottom line healthy—this means that they find little ways to charge you. For example, banks may charge you a fee when you open a savings account or if your account falls beneath a minimum amount. In addition, you don't get any tax breaks with a traditional savings account. Interest—or the money the bank pays you to keep your money there—is taxable on savings accounts. Here's the good news about these accounts, though—safety comes first. The FDIC insures bank accounts up to $100,000.

Bank Money Market Accounts: These are savings accounts that allow you to write a minimum of checks—usually three or so a month. You can also transfer money into a regular savings account, often automatically. As long as you maintain the required minimum, bank money market accounts usually pay higher interest than regular savings accounts. These minimums vary from bank to bank, as do interest rates and penalties for falling below the minimum.

Also, money market accounts may offer different rates of interest on different balances. For example, they may offer a tiered interest rate, which means that you earn the highest rate on your balance once you meet the minimum, or a blended rate, where you earn progressively more interest as you accumulate more money. The interest rates on money market accounts are typically half a percentage point below that of Treasury bills. Like traditional savings accounts, money market accounts are also federally insured, up to $100,000.

Certificates of Deposit: With a certificate of deposit, you simply invest a set amount of money—usually between $500 and $100,000—for a certain period of time (e.g., six months, one year, five years). You always get back the money you have invested, plus interest. The downside is that you cannot withdraw the money early without a penalty. You commit to a certain period of time, and the issuer commits to a certain rate of return. Generally, the longer the term of the CD, the higher the interest rate.

The benefits of investing in CDs include the following: Your account is insured for up to $100,000; the yield is usually higher than it is on other savings accounts; and no sales charges accompany the investment. The drawbacks are that your money is locked in at a specific rate, even if interest rates go up; you pay penalties if you withdraw early; and CD interest is taxable.

You can buy CDs through nearly any bank or broker, and

WALL STREET WISDOM ***It pays to get the best rate possible on your certificates of deposit (CDs.)***

1. *Check with at least three banks to see which has the highest rate. And you don't have to shop just in your area. You can also shop around the country. Rates are available in many of the personal finance magazines, such as* Your Money, Money, *and* Kiplingers, *and the Friday edition of the* Wall Street Journal. *Or check out the Bank Rate Monitor at P.O. Box 088888, North Palm Beach, FL 33408; 800-327-7717; 8 issues $48, and 52 issues $124, or on their Internet site at www.bankrate.com.*
2. *Find out how the interest is calculated. Of course, daily compounding is better than weekly or quarterly.*
3. *Make sure the quoted rate is for the duration of the CD. Some institutions will offer a high "introductory" rate, which drops after a short period.*
4. *Make sure you know the penalties for early withdrawal. Usually you want to keep your money in the CD for its duration. However, if CD rates increase significantly while you are holding a CD, you might be better off paying the early withdrawal penalty and reinvesting in a higher-rate CD.*

you can complete the entire transaction by mail. That means you can shop around. Even if you live in Alabama, and find the best CD rate in Santa Barbara, California, you can still do business.

Money Market Mutual Funds: As with any mutual fund, a money market fund pools your money with the money of thousands of other investors, and the combined assets are managed by a professional. Money market mutual funds aim for a higher yield than typical savings accounts do, but they entail less risk than an average mutual fund.

These funds invest in the *money market,* a term that refers to the way the government banks, large corporations, and securities dealers borrow and lend money for short periods of time—in other words, short-term debt securities. A money market mutual fund may invest in Treasury bills and notes, which are government IOUs; CDs, which are bank IOUs; and commercial paper, which are corporate IOUs.

Since the borrowers are good credit risk—usually Uncle Sam and huge, blue-chip companies—your risk is low. This is how they work: Your shares in a money market mutual fund are always worth $1 each. You earn money by interest. The money earned by the fund through these short-term loans, after expenses, is paid to the shareholders as interest, or *dividends.* The rate of interest fluctuates every day, and you can't predict how much interest you'll earn. But it's almost guaranteed that you won't *lose* money in these accounts. Although money market mutual funds are not insured, so far no one has lost money in them. Most money market mutual funds have a constant share price of $1, so it's easy to know how much your investment is worth at any time.

Many money market mutual funds require high minimum deposits—$1,000 is not an uncommon amount—but others let you in with less. You have to shop around. These funds are liquid—you have nearly immediate access to your money without penalty—and most allow you to write checks against your account. Many times these checks have to be large amounts, usually $500 or above. Be sure to get a no-load money market fund—some charge commissions.

Several types of money market mutual funds exist: General funds invest in nongovernment money market securities. Government-only funds invest in U.S. government or federal agency securities. These are backed by the U.S. government; they therefore tend to be less risky and offer a lower yield. Tax-free funds invest in short-term, tax-exempt municipal bonds. Since these are exempt from federal income tax (though not necessarily state and local), their yields are much lower. You can buy money market mutual funds through a broker, a discount broker, or directly from the mutual fund company (for a listing of these organizations, see chapter 5).

Where to Go to Get These Savings Accounts

Now that you've picked out some savings account options that appeal to you, where do you go to open these accounts? The following is a short list of your options.

Commercial Banks. Commercial banks are an old standby with a new twist. In addition to traditional services, such as checking and savings accounts, banks now offer everything from credit cards to mutual funds. That's because they are competing for customers with brokerage houses, credit unions, and private banks.

One big advantage to commercial banks is their convenience. If you sign up with a major commercial bank, chances are there will be a branch somewhere near where you work, shop, or play. That means you have easier access to your money, even if it's via Automatic Teller Machines (ATMs). Most commercial banks offer bank cards that allow you to use ATMs. These are good—you have access to your accounts at any time—and not so good; as we talked about in the last chapter, sometimes the last thing you want is access to your accounts. It's like having an automatic ice cream machine in your living room when you're on a diet.

Another big advantage is that, typically, the more money you keep in a bank, the less it costs you to take advantage of the bank's other options. And commercial banks usually offer a variety of options—everything from direct deposit capabilities to multiple-site ATMs to overdraft privileges. Commercial banks have gotten into the mutual fund game (and who hasn't?). We'll talk about this later, in our mutual fund chapter. Most bank accounts up to $100,000 are insured by the Federal Deposit Insurance Corporation (FDIC). These are pretty darn safe.

WALL STREET WISDOM: ***To be filed under the heading May you be so lucky as to have to be concerned about this one day. Keep in mind that it is the depositor—not the accounts—that are insured for up to $100,000 per bank by the FDIC. This means that if you have a $100,000 certificate of deposit and a $100,000 savings account with your local bank, you're only going to get $100,000 back if the bank folds.***

This is true if you have money spread out over different accounts, and even over different branches of the same bank. Changing your name or using a middle initial won't fool anybody.

However, if you're married, you have more options. You and your spouse will be insured for one individual account each, one joint account, two trust accounts, and one IRA account each. You're insured for all seven accounts—up to $700,000.

The downside to commercial banks is the fact that, well, they are so commercial. That means they're pretty impersonal—they may not recognize you, may not take special situations into account, and generally may not be all that pleasant to deal with. Also, commercial banks can charge you money in ways that are not so obvious. They can be tricky. They gouge you through fees. For instance, in 1992, the last year that these figures were available, the Consumer Federation of America reported that the nation's banks earned $3.67 billion in net profits from overdraft charges.

When you're heading to Wall Street, every nickel counts. So your best bet with any type of financial decision is always to shop around first.

Credit Unions. Credit unions are a great alternative to commercial banks. The first credit union was begun in Germany in the 1840s by a group of farmers. On this side of the Atlantic, they cropped up at the turn of the century to protect the common people from loan sharks and to give them savings and loan options. Over 12,000 exist in the United States.

Credit unions today, just like their forebears, are do-it-yourself banks, in a sense. They are formed among persons with a common bond, usually an occupation, an association, or a community. Credit union members pool their financial resources and make low-interest loans to each other. Unlike banks, they are nonprofit, and therefore exempt from federal income tax.

In addition, they usually charge fewer fees than banks do. How can they do this? The same reason they're exempt from federal income tax: Credit unions are nonprofit, and they use their fees more to organize their structures rather than to make more money. Most accounts in credit unions are insured up to $100,000 by the National Credit Union Administration (NCUA), a federal agency that supervises and examines insured credit unions. Others are cooperatively insured; that is, they form their own insurance companies.

Although most credit unions are insured, double-check this before you choose one. In addition to high-interest savings, lower-interest loans, fewer fees, and low minimum balance requirements, credit unions often offer perks such as discounted AAA memberships, discounted movie tickets, or warehouse club membership passes.

Take a look at this: In 1996, a general survey of banks and credit unions showed that average credit union checking account fees were approximately \$3.90 per month, compared to \$5.80 at a bank. Credit union money market accounts paid an average return of 3.8 percent, while banks were paying an average of 2.4 percent. Even credit card rates were lower: Credit unions offered an average of 12.8 percent, while banks offered cards that averaged rates of 18 percent.

What this means for you, the individual investor, is a place to park your savings that may offer higher interest rates, or

WALL STREET WISDOM: ***When shopping for a bank or credit union, ask the following questions.***

What are the fees for a checking account?
Is there a per-check fee?
What is the charge for insufficient funds?
What is the stop-payment charge?
What is the charge for overdrafts?
What is the rate of their credit card?
How many ATMs do they own? What is the fee?
How often is interest compounded?
Do they offer discounts for seniors? Or free checking if you sign up for direct deposit of your salary or Social Security check?
Do they offer Internet banking?

a place to get loans that have lower interest rates. However, you'll usually find fewer branch locations, less opportunity for a home mortgage, and limited ATM access. Call the Credit Union National Association (CUNA) at 800-358-5710 or visit their Web page at http://www.cuna.org for the site nearest you.

Mutual Funds Companies. Mutual funds companies now offer banking services, although these services may be limited. Money market funds are offered to give investors a way to accumulate money until they have enough to invest in regular mutual funds. These accounts also offer safety. As we mentioned above, money market funds are invested in money market securities, which are short-term debts with high liquidity, including certificates of deposits and Treasury bills. In other words, they are pretty safe, and typically you have check-writing privileges, usually with minimums higher than other accounts require—$500 or so. They offer competitive interest rates—often double that of the average bank savings account.

These funds pay interest and offer the same liquidity as banks savings, checking, and money market accounts. However, they are not insured by the federal government. Also, some mutual funds companies offer savings and checking accounts in conjunction with your investment accounts. Or you can open a brokerage account that has a money market account attached. These brokerage accounts offer unlimited check-writing privileges and ATM cards, and you can purchase stocks, bonds, and mutual funds, all in one account. These cash-management accounts are convenient, and they can be a great way to keep your money on hand while you invest and reinvest. Keep in mind that some brokerage accounts do have fees and minimum balance requirements.

It's a buyer's market. So shop around. You may use one situation for your savings and checking accounts, another for your CD account, and a third for a money market account. Remember, a penny saved is a couple of pennies toward your $5 a day.

WALL STREET WISDOM: ***For mortgage assistance, consider using services that help you survey commercial banks, mortgage companies, and credit unions. HSH Associates (800-873-2837) and National Mortgage Weekly (216-273-6605) offer such services.***

PROTECT YOUR ASSETS WITH INSURANCE

You can ruin your investments and your financial future if you're not protected in the event of a health crisis, early death in the family, or disability. To protect yourself, you need insurance. What does the average investor need? Basically, you want to insure yourself against anything that can lead to a financial catastrophe. Period. Anything else is negligible.

That means that you need health insurance. That's a given. Disability? Yes: If you're under forty-five years old, your odds of becoming disabled are greater than your odds of dying. And life insurance? Definitely, if you have people who are dependent on you. Let's go through these one by one.

Health Insurance

Most Americans are offered a health plan through their job—usually part of a group plan. This is usually the best way, because group plans tend to be the cheapest, and the most forgiving. For one thing, group plans accept those with preexisting conditions much more easily than individual health insurance plans do.

What happens if you're self-employed, or otherwise unable to get health insurance through your workplace? You'll have to shop around. Check with an insurance broker. Also, look into professional and civic organizations. For instance, if you are a self-employed carpenter, your town may have a carpenter's association that offers a group insurance plan. If you can't find any viable individual health plans on your own, consider part-time employment. Many part-time jobs now offer health benefits. And at age sixty-five and beyond, you are eligible for Medicare, the government-run insurance program

When choosing a health policy, be aware of your choices. These include Health Maintenance Organizations (HMOs), Preferred Provider Organizations (PPOs), and open-choice plans. With HMOs you are limited to the health care providers within a network. PPOs are similar to HMOs, except you usually have the option of going outside your network. You may have to pay a bit more, however. For example, if you really like Dr. Smith's treatment of your asthma, but he's outside of your PPO network, you can still visit him and get reimbursed for part of the visit. (If you were with an HMO and he was outside of your network, none of the visit would be paid for.) Therefore, if you have primary health care providers you really like, check first to see if they are within the HMO or PPO network. Otherwise, you may want to choose the open-choice policy, where you can go to whomever you want, but your premiums are generally more expensive.

What should you look for in a health insurance policy? A reasonable lifetime maximum—that is, a dollar amount limit for lifetime coverage that seems high enough. This could mean several million dollars, since health care costs can be extraordinary. Also look at your co-payment and deductible options. Most HMOs don't have co-payments or deductibles; you merely pay a set amount per office visit.

The higher your *deductibles* (the money you pay before your coverage kicks in—usually $250, $500, or $1,000 per year), the lower your insurance premiums. When considering

WALL STREET WISDOM: ***If you're having trouble getting health insurance coverage, try the following:***

1. **Obtain a copy of your medical information file:** *Write the Medical Information Bureau at P.O. Box 105, Essex Station, Boston, MA 02112 or call 617-426-3660. Check to make sure that the information listed on your report is correct. You have the right to request that any errors be fixed; however, the burden of proof is on you, including contacting pertinent physicians. Ask the insurer why you were denied. They may have misinterpreted some of the information on your report—or the information may have been wrong.*
2. **Shop around:** *If you do have a preexisting condition, you may find it harder to find an insurer, but not all insurers judge on the same basis. You may be able to find an insurer to cover you, although your rates may be higher because of a condition, or they may include a "rider" that covers everything but your preexisting condition. An independent agent, or someone who sells a variety of policies from a variety of companies, may be a good place to try.*
3. **Check out civic and professional organizations:** *Since your best bet is often a group plan, see if any of the organizations to which you belong offer a health plan.*
4. **Look to your state:** *Many states offer pools that insure people unable to get coverage elsewhere. Check your local phone book and look under the state government section. Call the state's insurance department to see if they offer this.*

your overall choices, weigh how much money you'll have to pay outright, including deductibles and co-payments, against your premium costs.

You also want a policy that is *guaranteed renewable,* so you aren't left in the lurch if you develop a medical condition that costs a lot of money to treat and your insurance company decides they'd rather not be responsible for your future medical bills.

Disability Insurance

If you're under age forty-five, your chances of becoming disabled are greater than your chances of dying. Most disabilities—or the inability to work—occur because of common medical conditions such as arthritis, heart conditions, or back problems.

The sole purpose of disability insurance is to protect your salary. In other words, if you can't work because you've been hurt, or you become ill, disability insurance guarantees that you'll be able to pay your rent, or your mortgage, and support yourself or your family. So, in a sense, it protects your greatest asset—your income potential.

Most people can obtain their disability insurance through work. Again, if you are self-employed or work for an employer who does not offer disability insurance, then you need to look around for yourself.

Q. How much do you need?

A: Basically, you need enough disability insurance to enable you to pay your bills until you're back on your feet. Look for a policy that will replace your after-tax salary—or at least 80 percent of it. You also need to decide for how long you'll want these benefits. If you are near retirement, or you have someone who can help support you if you become disabled, you can choose a policy of a shorter duration. Obviously, these are cheaper.

Q: What else should you look for?

A: Consider a policy that is noncancelable and guaranteed renewable. The last thing you want is a disability policy that can be canceled because of poor health. Check out your insurance company's financial stability. You want a company that can pay your claims if you do become disabled.

You will have the option of choosing a waiting period, which is the time from the onset of your disability to when the benefits kick in. You can usually choose anywhere from thirty days to two years. The longer you can wait, the lower your deductibles. Make sure it's realistic, though. If you have only three months' living expenses in a savings account, you'll be hard-pressed to survive for a year without a salary.

Q: Where do you get disability insurance?

A: If you cannot buy disability insurance through your job, then check out professional and civic organizations. Again, group plans are usually your best bet. If you're looking for disability insurance on your own, bypassing an agent may save you money. Direct-buying services are springing up across the country, where you can purchase disability and life insurance directly and by phone.

Life Insurance

Combine a fear of death with an aversion to salespeople, and you have one of the main reasons people avoid protecting

WALL STREET WISDOM: ***The following services offer competitively priced disability insurance policies.***

1. *Fee-For-Service (800-874-5602)*
2. *USAA (800-622-3699)*
3. *Insurance Quote (800-972-1104)*
4. *Select Quote (800-343-1985)*

their families through life insurance. On the flip side, life insurance is perhaps one of the most *overused* insurances around. There you have it. The people who need life insurance don't always get it, and the ones who don't need it are snapping it up.

Who really needs life insurance? You do, if you have people dependent on you. Otherwise, you're paying a lot of money toward fees, not toward investment. You see, you can break down life insurance policies into the following categories: Mortality expense, or how much money the life insurance company will pay your beneficiaries when you die; commissions, or how much the salesperson who sold you the policy gets; operating expense, or how much the insurance company gets; and cash value, which, depending on what type of policy you buy, is the accumulated earnings of the policy, if any, after expenses are paid.

Some people use life insurance just to ensure that their dependents will have money if they die prematurely. Others use life insurance as an investment. Basically, two types of life insurance exist, with nuances in each category: Whole life, or cash life, provides death benefits *and* has an investment component. Term life provides death benefits, period. Here's a rundown of your options. A basic rule of thumb says that if you don't have people dependent on you for your salary, you probably could find a better way than life insurance to invest your money.

Term life insurance is the most straightforward life insurance you can buy. Basically, you pay money to be insured for a specific amount of time. You usually buy it for a year, five years, or more. When you stop paying, your coverage ends. Your premiums, or what you pay to own the insurance, do not accumulate in any way. You are simply paying for the insurance. Two types of term insurance exist: level and renewable. Level term is when you lock in a premium rate for the specified term. Annual renewable policies can be renewed each year, but with increasingly expensive premiums. Regardless, term insurance is usually the least expensive of your life insurance options. And you can take the money you'll save by buying term and investing it in the stock market for a higher rate of return.

WALL STREET WISDOM: ***If you're shopping around for life insurance, it makes sense to know who pays the lowest rates. (As if you needed another reason for clean living.)***

You'll pay the lowest rates if you have . . .

Been a nonsmoker for the past four years.

Been the recipient of no more than three moving violations in the past three years.

Been DUI-free.

Blood pressure below 140/90 without medication.

No serious illnesses.

Weight under the maximum on company chart.

No more than one death from heart disease before age 60 in your immediate family.

Cholesterol/hdl cholesterol ratios that do not exceed five.

Traditional whole life insurance provides insurance coverage *and* tax-deferred savings. You pay premiums, which are usually much higher than term, throughout your life. These remain the same for the life of the policy. Not only are you guaranteed lifelong coverage, but you can also build up equity in your life insurance policy (after the expenses and commissions are paid off).Your premiums for traditional whole life insurance go toward paying company and policy expenses and salesperson commissions; the rest is invested in the stock market, in stocks and bonds. Traditional whole life insurance policies are invested approximately 75 percent in bonds and 25 percent in stocks. Therefore, the return is usually lower than a more stock-oriented portfolio, but it's easier to guarantee a general rate of return.

Universal life insurance is also a cash policy, which means that it's both an investment and an insurance policy. However, with a universal life policy, you have the option of making flexible premium payments, based on your contract terms.

Variable life insurance gives you investment options: You can choose how your premium dollars are invested. Therefore, your cash value and death benefits will fluctuate, depending on the underlying value of the portfolio.

The plus to whole life policies is that you are accumulating cash value. Although the rate of return is usually significantly lower than the stock market (by approximately 3 percentage points over the long run), insurance companies can usually offer you a guaranteed range of return.

Be aware, however, that a good portion of your initial premium payments goes toward commissions and expenses. Therefore, if you want to cancel your policy within the first ten years or so, you'll probably end up losing money.

Some investors see this as a motivation to keep investing in their life insurance policy. In addition, with whole life policies, you lock into a life insurance rate for life, which means that if you are planning on having dependents someday, your rate will most likely be lower than if you bought your policy at a later day. And you're already in: no rejecting you or hiking the premium rates for preexisting conditions—the most dreaded words in any would-be insured person's vocabulary.

Also, you can borrow against a whole life plan, although you may get charged interest. But if you decide not to pay back the money, you're out only the interest, minus death benefits. The most famous adage concerning life insurance is, Buy term and invest the rest. But it's a personal decision.

WALL STREET WISDOM: ***If you're unsure whether to cash in your cash-value policy and buy term and invest the rest, contact the Insurance Group of the Consumer Federation of America. They'll analyze your rate of return and tell you what you'd have to earn while investing in order to beat it.***

The service costs $40 for the first policy and $30 for each additional policy. Write the Consumer Federation of America at 1424 16th Street, NW, Suite 604, Washington, D.C. 20036; 202-387-0087.

How much life insurance do you need? Your dependents will need the following if you die: emergency fund money, funeral costs, and medical bills. They'll also need money for taxes, mortgage, education, and day-to-day living expenses. Other sources of support for your dependents are your survivor's salary, investments, and Social Security benefits.

You can buy life insurance through a broker (someone who sells a variety of policies from a variety of companies) or an agent, who sells from one company only. A new trend is insurance telephone brokerage services, where you can dial an 800 number and get a policy—bypassing agents and brokers and their fees.

WALL STREET WISDOM: ***Here's a list of insurance you never need to buy:***

1. ***Life insurance for a child.*** *Unless your child is supporting your family, there's no real reason to buy this. Take the money you'd spend on the premiums, and invest it in a mutual fund for the child instead.*
2. ***Cancer insurance.*** *Your health insurance should already cover you for major illnesses. If it doesn't, shop around some more.*
3. ***Flight insurance.*** *Most of what you pay for flight insurance goes to pay marketing expenses—and line the pockets of the insurance company. Only a small portion is paid out in benefits.*
4. ***Car rental insurance.*** *Only consider this insurance if you're not covered on your coexisting car insurance policy or through your credit card. Remember, the best insurance here is not monetary: Drive safely and buckle up.*

Other Insurance

Two other kinds of insurance exist that are good for the small investor. The first is homeowner's or renter's insurance. This protects your residence from damage—and liability. If you own a home, chances are you were required to buy homeowner's insurance. Even if you're not, it's always a good idea.

Auto insurance is required by law in most states. You always want to protect your assets, so the amount and type of auto insurance that you buy should reflect this. For example, as your car ages, you may want to raise the deductibles, or even consider dropping your collision insurance altogether. That way, you'll be covered by law, but you can't use your insurance money to fix your car. If you're driving a ten-year-old clunker, it may not matter.

WALL STREET WISDOM: ***If you want to slash your car insurance payments by up to 20 percent annually, arm yourself with this knowledge when it's time to buy or renew.***

You're likely to get a discount, if the following is true for you:

1. *You graduated from a public university in the same state in which you're buying the insurance.*
2. *You bought a new car with antilock brakes, air bags, or an anti-theft system.*
3. *You drive less than 7,500 miles per year.*
4. *You are enrolled in, or have recently completed, a defensive driving class.*

Last Will and Testament

If you're married, and you or your spouse dies without a will, it automatically puts the surviving spouse in financial jeopardy. On top of the trauma of loss, the survivor will also have to deal with the trauma of inaccessible assets while the estate is being settled. The survivor may have trouble meeting bills during this time, and, worse, may lose a portion of her inheritance to the state. Do all your loved ones a favor; always keep an updated will.

***WALL STREET WISDOM:** Before you buy insurance, do your homework, and check out the stability of the insurance company. The following companies offer rating services. You can either subscribe to their ratings, or look them up in your local library. The rating system is not unlike a school grading system: An A is excellent; C is not so great.*

Each company has its own way to rate, and will explain this in its rating booklets. It's a good idea to cross-check companies with a minimum of two rating services.

1. *Best's Insurance Reports*
   A.M. Best Co.
   Oldwick, NJ 08858
   1-900-555-2378

2. *Standard & Poor's Insurance Rating Service*
   25 Broadway
   New York, NY 10004
   1-212-208-8000

3. *Weiss Research, Inc.*
   2200 North Florida Mango Rd.
   West Palm Beach, FL 33409
   1-800-289-92222

ASK A FINANCIAL PLANNER

In this financial planning session, Darryl Reed examined the clients' insurance and savings needs.

Darryl Reed speaks: Joe has access to health, life, and disability insurance at work, and he is taking advantage of the health and disability options. His pay reflects what is left after these insurances have been paid for. Joe is particularly smart because he has chosen to take advantage of the disability insurance option. This is one of the most important types of insurance—and one of the most commonly overlooked.

Life insurance is not a major concern at this point for Joe, since he is not married and does not have any family members that rely on his income-producing capacity. However, looking at the big picture, we do see an area of concern. Joe has to learn how to save. It's one of the biggest problems that people face—especially people Joe's age. He has done a good job of remaining debt free—excluding his low-interest school loan—which will help enormously as he begins to save and invest.

Joe may want to begin to contribute $36 per month to a money market account to build up his cash reserves. Since he has a credit union through his work, he would do well to look there; interest rates are usually higher than money market accounts available through banks. Although it is typically recommended that each person accumulate three to six months of bill-paying capability, Joe may be able to get by with less, since he feels very secure about his job. Once he does get to an adequate level of emergency savings—let's say several thousand dollars—he might then look at diversifying his growing portfolio of investments.

• First and foremost, David and Tess should look at the group life insurance that is available through their employers. They face potential financial ruin should something happen to either of them. An important point to consider on the insurance side is not to purchase life insurance for Sonny, their child. Many parents fall prey to this emotional sales pitch. The fact that David is taking advantage of disability insurance through his employer is good. As we know, most people miss covering this risk.

David and Tess also need to beef up their emergency cash reserves. They can start to save a portion of $185 free cash flow they have each month, and add to the $2,000 they have. However, they should not delay starting to invest just because their emergency reserve is not completely where they would like to see it. With their investment goals, they need to begin to invest.

Between $5,000 and $7,000 might be a good start for an emergency fund, based on the stability of their positions and the fact that they both have large families nearby that may be able to assist them should an emergency crop up. They should also consider a home equity line of credit that they can draw against in the case of emergencies. Since they have been in their home for eight years, and since they used most of the money they received from their wedding as a down payment, they are starting to have substantial equity built up. Now is the time also to see if they can discontinue paying their private mortgage insurance (PMI).

The good thing about Tess and David is that they can probably get their new car within a reasonable amount of time since their current car payment will end in eighteen months. In order to stay within their spending range, they may have to look at a less expensive car, or one that is slightly used. Once they have the type of car picked out, they should consider shopping via the Internet in order to get the best deal. AutoMall.USA.net might be a good place to start comparing. They can also check out Autobytel.com.

• Carla is doing much better now that she has addressed her spending habits. They were draining her resources, pushing her backward instead of forward. Now she has a clearly defined plan and an overall direction in mind. She has discussed with her children what she is trying to do. Even her daughter, Lauren, who is ten years old, wants to help. She said that she would get a paper route to help the family save for a new house. Getting the whole family involved in the plan is important. Her son Blake, who is eight years old, said that he'll think about not having to have as many toys as his friends.

Getting out of debt shouldn't be a problem for Carla now that she has her spending under control. She has agreed to cut up all but one or two of her credit cards. She is also looking for a card that will allow her to roll her $2,000 balance over at a low initial first-year rate, possibly 5 or 6 percent. That may free up $10 more a month. Getting out of debt should be a priority for Carla; she should set aside $50 per month to pay her credit card balance.

Carla should also set aside $50 a month initially as an emergency fund. After a cash reserve of approximately $5,000 has been attained, she can then start to consider adding that to her "new home savings." A money market is a good place to start to accumulate cash. Depending on how long it takes before she has enough to make a down payment, she might consider getting a fixed income mutual fund or purchasing a short-term Treasury. Either will pay more than the money market, and she can purchase the Treasury through the Treasury Direct program for no transaction fee.

Earning more money is the bottom line. Carla will have to investigate ways to earn more money if she wants to realize her goals of owning a home, saving enough for retirement, and sending her children to college. She has had an interest, she says, in selling Avon products. Besides being able to create an additional income for herself, she may find that increasing her circle of contacts could improve her chances of finding a better primary job.

Also, Carla should consider talking to her employer about the possibility of a group life insurance policy through work. She may find that her employer, Tom, at Luscious Landscaping, Inc., has already been thinking about this. He may find a way to save money for himself, too. Carla might consider doing a little of the groundwork before she goes to Tom. This will save him time, as well as make Carla an even more valuable asset in Tom's mind.

• John went back to his company, Hart's Brewery, and asked them to recalculate his actual pension benefit. He had a feeling that he wasn't receiving the correct amount. Sure enough, Hart's Brewery was wrong by $30 per month. After the pension change and expense adjustment, Marge and John now have $150 per month in excess cash flow. They also received a lump sum of $600, which was the underpayment of John's pension over the past year or so.

Still, John and Marge really want to do more than their finances will allow them to do during retirement. Although they've never had an extravagant lifestyle, they've never been sit-around-the-house-type of people. They simply want to be able to travel a little, especially to see their grandchildren who live in Seattle, eat out when they like, and not have to worry about paying day-to-day bills.

We talked about part-time work. John has extensive experience in many areas of maintenance. When John was in the navy, he was trained as a ship maintenance technician. Plumbing and electrical work are almost second nature to him. In fact, when John was released from service with the navy, he originally started working with Hart's in the factory maintenance section. Even though John worked in sales for the past thirty years, he feels that he has extensive experience in home remodeling and maintenance.

Marge has been a homemaker most of her life. Raising three children, running the household, and volunteering time to the local hospital have been more than a full-time job. She has always been active in the community, organizing the local summer festival and hospital holiday fund-raiser. From this she has gained valuable organizational and management skills. She has also made a lot of contacts with business owners.

John and Marge have decided that working part-time is probably in their best interest. Although they can make it on the money they have, they want more of a cushion if something unforeseen happens. John has decided to work three days per week (about twenty hours) at the local Home Depot, a home improvement/remodeling store. John figures this will bring in about $150 a week after taxes. Marge is still looking, but she has several offers for an administrative assistant position with local business owners. She is leaning toward becoming a tutor at the local community college for foreign students who are struggling with English.

I asked John and Marge to evaluate their health care coverage. They are not exactly sure what is covered under their retirement plan from Hart's. Although the company has covered any problems they have had since retirement and certainly provided great medical benefits when John worked there, they need to look into this.

They should also look at how selling their home may impact their lifestyle. Since their children have all moved closer to the city, they may want to consider selling their home and purchasing something smaller in the years ahead (perhaps after they decide to quit working part-time). Although they have expressed an interest in remaining in their current home, at some point the largeness may become an issue. Since their home is currently valued at $220,000, and they could buy a nice condominium for $120,000, the gain they may receive from this house, in conjunction with the capital gains exclusion, could add $100,000 or more to the retirement picture.

Even though Marge and John take good care of themselves—they eat right, exercise, and are active, and plan on another twenty or so active years—they should update their wills. This has been on their lists for a long time, but they never seem to get around to it, even though Lorraine down the street is their attorney.

Having a will in place is the basic building block of any estate plan. It's doubtful that their total estate will be over $600,000, so the taxes would be offset by the Unified Estate and Gift Tax Credit. However, just making sure that their property goes to their family is important to them.

They also need to give each other and a trusted family member the healthcare power of attorney. Making your wishes known while you still can is important to most people. They can probably have Lorraine draft this up when they see her for the will. Actually, this is something that everyone should consider.

In terms of spending, they want to make sure that

they are taking advantage of any discount programs that are available for seniors. They might find that the insurance, utility, or cable company has slight breaks for them. They have to also remember to ask at hotels, restaurants, and other service providers. Linking up with a seniors group such as the AARP makes sense so that they can take advantage of.

WALL STREET REVISITED: Checklist for chapter 2

1. *Your first step in investing is protecting your assets. First, you need to make sure that you have an accessible savings account for emergencies. One of the biggest dangers to your investment portfolio is interruption—and debt. A solid savings account helps to protect you against both.*
2. *Shop around for the best deal in savings accounts. You have a lot of choices today, including bank savings accounts, credit union accounts, money market accounts, and CDs, to name a few. Remember, you always want to find the highest-quality deal for the least amount of money. It's a buyer's market.*
3. *Make sure you protect yourself with appropriate insurance. The basic coverage will include health and disability insurance. If you have people dependent on you, you'll probably need life insurance as well.*
4. *If you do not receive insurance coverage through work, shop around for the best rates possible. Overinsuring yourself can be nearly as detrimental as underinsuring yourself. Avoid anything that needlessly takes money from you and your investment plan.*
5. *Make sure that you have an updated will.*

THREE

Welcome to Wall Street

The New York Stock Exchange has announced that it will begin quoting stock prices in decimals instead of fractions by January 2000. After considering this issue for quite some time today, I have concluded that I have absolutely no idea what this means.

—Comic Bill Shein

WALL STREET NAVIGATOR: Finding your way around chapter 3

Welcome to Wall Street: History and facts
Who's who in investments: Stocks, bonds, and cash investments
Crash course in economics
Risk and investing

Investing can be like closing your eyes and jumping into a lake. You hope that the water's deep enough, and you hope that the lifeguards are doing their duty. But really, when it comes right down to it, it's rather a leap of faith.

You can buttress this faith, however, with preparation. The first two chapters of this book were about preparation. You had to trim the fat from your budget to find the $5 a day to invest. You had to set goals. You had to open, or add to, an accessible savings account so that you had money for emergencies. Also, you made sure that you were adequately covered by insurance—health, life, and disability—so that your investing path wasn't interrupted by life's inevitabilities.

Here's another way to prepare: by gaining a basic knowledge of Wall Street. One of the most important things you can do for yourself is to have a solid understanding of Wall Street *before* you actually get there. Investing is more than following the advice in a book. It's a lifetime commitment: You have to continually make new investment decisions and monitor your portfolio as it grows. Knowledge helps to reduce the inevitable risks of investing. In this chapter, we're going to give you a bird's-eye view of Wall Street—all the basics.

Pack up the kids, and let's go.

ON THE ROAD TO WALL STREET

Hop on the tour bus to Wall Street. Take a look around. Where exactly are you? Although Wall Street is a real street located at the southern tip of Manhattan, it's also a concept, the nickname given to the financial and business center of New York—and, as computers and modems have shrunk the investing world, to the stock market in general.

The original Wall Street was named after a wall built by Dutch settlers in 1653 to protect New York City, some say, from pirate attacks, others say, to protect the city's sheep and goats. Today, you won't find sheep or goats, but you will find bulls and bears, but we'll talk about that later. Eventually, the wall came down, but they memorialized it by naming the street that replaced it *Wall Street.* In 1792, the first meeting of the New York Stock Exchange took place, right there on Wall Street, with the traders sitting on wooden tables underneath a buttonwood tree.

Take a look ahead. You'll see the current New York Stock Exchange (NYSE) and the American Stock Exchange (AMEX), two of the largest and most important of the world's more than 140 stock exchanges. In 1792, the NYSE was a place to trade furs, tobacco, and spices. It's grown. Today, brokers trade the *stock* of clothing manufacturers, tobacco companies, and food corporations, and much, much more. Millions of dollars' worth of transactions happen every day. The companies that list on the NYSE are usually the biggest and best-known companies, those whose stocks are known as blue-chip stocks. (Just like a blue chip in poker, this term means quality on Wall Street.) The companies listed on the AMEX tend to be smaller and younger.

With all the fuss about the NYSE and AMEX, you may be surprised to hear that the majority of U.S. stocks aren't even traded through exchanges. Instead they're traded on the over-the-counter market, OTC, which is an electronic marketplace. Most OTC stocks are traded through NASDAQ, the National Association of Securities Dealers Automated Quotation System. Usually, OTC stocks are from the smallest, youngest companies. Increasingly, however, larger and more established companies are choosing to stay on the OTC.

STOCK NEWS

So, what is a stock? Quite simply, a stock is part ownership, or a share, in a company. It's a piece of the pie. Companies sell stock so that they have capital, or money with which to grow. Companies can either borrow money from banks, or they can issue stocks and bonds to the public. Alexander Graham Bell, for example, needed money for a little project he was working on—the telephone. His bank loan application was rejected. He looked to private investors. He was able to find investors who thought he could make a go of it. So when he did, these investors, who owned stock in his company—now the American Telephone and Telegraph (AT&T)—became quite rich. Since you become part-owner of a company and gain *equity* in it when you buy stock, stocks are also known as *equities.*

When a company first offers stock, it's said to be going public. This is called the Initial Public Offering (IPO). You can make a lot of money if you buy a good stock at its offering price (think Microsoft). However, it's very hard for individual investors to get in on the ground floor. For one thing, good IPOs are usually snapped up by mutual fund managers, institutional investors (those who manage pensions, for example), and other industry insiders. Also, offering prices can rise rapidly, and you can miss the boat. Anyway, if you're a beginning investor you might be wise to avoid brand-new stock unless you're really familiar with the company—and have a way of getting in. An example of this would be the stock of the company for which you work. Otherwise, it's pretty speculative.

When a company does offer stock, it gives up some of its decision-making rights in exchange for the money it receives. As a stockholder, you can attend shareholder meetings and vote on how the company is run. You also share directly in the success—or failure—of a company (not all companies become AT&T).

You can make money two ways through stock. One way is through dividends, or periodic payments of cash made from the company's earnings. You usually receive dividend payments four times a year, and the board of directors can increase, decrease, or cancel these dividends at any time. For example, if the company does well, it may decide to increase

WALL STREET WISDOM: ***Eighty percent of all American companies do not sell stock. Why? Because they're privately, not publicly, owned. These companies are usually small, mom-and-pop operations that have raised money on their own. Not all privately owned companies are small, however. Mars Candy is a privately owned company that has made billionaires out of the Mars family.***

Companies actually need permission from the government to sell stock. Otherwise, it would be hard to regulate trading. The process is called becoming incorporated. Therefore, corporations are another word for companies that can sell stock. These are public companies.

Closely held companies, a third group, are owned partly by investors. Usually these investors are family members or close friends of the business owner.

its dividend payments. Some companies consistently pay dividends; others never do. Stocks that consistently pay dividends, such as utility stocks, are known as income stocks. Companies that pay little or no dividends are known as growth stocks. Why would you buy these? Because price appreciation can be great.

Appreciation is the second way that you can make money through stocks. Simply put, appreciation is when a stock goes up in value. So if you buy Stock AAA today at $14 a share, and in five years it is worth $50 a share, you'll make a nice little profit when you sell it.

You may be surprised to hear that many investors today aren't individuals. Stocks are also bought by institutions, such as employee pension fund and mutual fund investors. Since these investors have large sums of money to invest—sometimes hundreds of millions of dollars—their patterns of buying and selling can affect market prices.

Sometimes, if a company wants to entice new investors, it will initiate a stock split. It's not rocket science. If the stock splits two for one, the stock is half its original price. Voila! Cheaper prices (although the exact same value) may attract bargain hunters. Interestingly, often a stock split will boost the value of a stock. A split calls attention to the company, and often results in increased buying. Also, small investors are often attracted to the reduced price per share.

BUYING STOCK

Thanks to the Securities and Exchange Commission (SEC), it's now easier (read: more affordable) for small investors to buy individual stocks. In 1974, the SEC deregulated the retail brokerage industry. This opened the door for competitive brokerage rates. Before 1974, you had to hire a stockbroker, usually at a major brokerage firm such as Merrill Lynch, Smith Barney, or E.F. Hutton, in order to buy stocks. These firms' stockbrokers gave advice—they told their clients when to buy and when to sell their stock—and helped their clients manage their portfolios.

However, most of these stockbrokers earned their money based on commission—that is, the amount of trading that they did. For example, buying 200 shares of a $25 stock will cost you between $120 and $140 in commissions at the major brokerage firms. So sometimes it was in the broker's interest—not the client's—to do certain transactions.

With the advent of deregulation came discount brokers—firms such as Charles Schwab, Jack White, Fidelity, and others—which allow investors to buy and sell stock without high transaction fees. For example, the same transaction as above—buying 200 shares of a $25 stock—will cost only $60 to $80 at a discount broker.

How can discount brokers get away with charging less? Simple. They offer no, or little, advice. Discount brokers hire order clerks, who are paid straight salary, instead of commissioned brokers. No conflict of interest exists. However, this means that the investor has to know what's going on. You have to do your own homework, and make your own decisions.

The lastest wave in discount brokerage is online brokers. The average trade costs less than twenty dollars, and while no advice is given, you can research investments online.

There's another trend in buying stocks: buying directly from the company. These are usually called Dividend Reinvestment Plans, or DRIPs. You can get some of the best deals around through this setup because you may be paying no fees whatsoever. We'll talk about this more in chapter 6.

CHOOSING STOCKS

How do you know how valuable a stock is? The funny thing about stocks is that they have no inherent worth. No one comes down from on high and says, "This is worth a lot," "This stock is worth little." It's all about perception. If a stock is perceived to be valuable, and people buy it, then it is. Of course, when you buy a stock, you're hoping that others will find it valuable, too. That means that the price will go up, and that you'll make money when you decide to sell it.

What are some of the indicators of value in a stock—or what makes investors value a stock? How well a company is doing, for one. How well the industry is doing is another indicator. The general state of the economy motivates investors, as do societal trends. When choosing stocks, most experienced investors use either a *fundamental* analysis, which

Wall Street Wisdom: ***The following are the four biggest mistakes an investor can make, according to Dave Cox, a portfolio manager and director of research at The Chicago Trust Company.***

1. **Market timing:** *Market timing means trying to anticipate market trends, and entering and exiting the stock market accordingly. Don't try this at home—you'll only end up outsmarting yourself. You want to have an investment plan, not a speculatory attitude. Your own goals and investment time line are your biggest concerns, not what stocks will go up when.*
2. **Too much debt:** *You've heard it already in this book, and you'll hear it again: If you're spending valuable money on interest, you'll find it very hard to get out of the hole and compile a portfolio that works for your life goals.*

   Credit cards are for emergencies and convenience, and loans are for big-ticket items such as housing, cars, and education.
3. **Overinsuring (especially life insurance):** *You really have no need for life insurance if you don't have dependents, and even then, your best bet is probably to buy term. You can get a better rate investing your money in the stock market. Period. Besides, if you do a good job investing, you'll get to the point where life insurance is irrelevant.*
4. **Spending rather than saving: either saving too little or starting too late:** *I know, you've heard this too many times to count, but a penny saved really is a penny earned.*

   And if you waste valuable expendable cash on expendable items, you've lost precious time in the stock market. Remember the chart in chapter 1: for every missed year, you have that much more money to invest a month to get to where you want to go.

   Even $5 makes a huge difference. Money is important from the first day you get it.

includes looking at a company's current and anticipated earnings, the strength of its management, its competition, and new market potential; or *technical* analysis, in which price trends, cyclical movements of stocks, industries, and the market are considered. Some investors look at both.

Many investors use their intuition; for example, they may decide to invest in their favorite store or product. It's a good idea to use your intuition, but back it up with analysis—fundamental or technical.

You can find the information for analyzing stocks—for instance, company earnings, dividend announcements, or merger news—in the business sections of newspapers, business papers, and business periodicals such as *Barron's,* the *Wall Street Journal, Money,* and *Your Money* magazines. (See resource guide on page *239.*) A company releases its earnings, or profits, four times a year. This is probably the most indicative factor of stock performance. Of course, the companies themselves can provide you with important information through their prospectuses and annual reports.

BOND NEWS

Two types of securities exist in the financial world: stocks (or equity) and bonds (or debt). Unlike stocks, which give you a piece of ownership in a company, a bond is a type of IOU. When you buy a bond, you are basically lending money, usually to a company or government agency. This issuer, as these borrowers are called, agrees to repay your loan at its full value (the principal). The issuer also agrees to pay you interest. And he agrees to pay the interest at regular intervals, and to repay your loan in full at a set date. The interest rate is known as the coupon rate and is usually paid every six months. All of this is set up in advance, before you purchase the bond.

Bonds also differ from stocks in that they are fixed-income investments. That means you know how much money you're supposed to receive (as long as the issuer remains in business) in interest. It's regular, set income. You'll usually want to balance your portfolio, or collection of investments, with both stocks and bonds. Stocks offer a real growth opportunity—they have a historic return of 10 percent—and bonds can offer stability.

Usually interest on bonds is paid every six months. Typically, the longer the bond life, the higher the interest rate, because the borrower is tying up your money for a longer time. And you need to get paid for the inflation and interest-rate risk over a longer period.

So who issues bonds? Uncle Sam and its agencies are the largest issuers. Treasuries, as they're called, are the safest investment around because they're backed by the "full faith and credit" of the U.S. government. Local government gets in the game as well. If your town needs a new bridge or library, for example, it can issue bonds, called municipals, to raise money. A big difference between the two types of bonds is that municipal bonds are not taxable. Therefore, you earn even more money.

Another major classification is corporate bonds, which are issued by companies as a means of obtaining financing. These tend to be riskier, because they're not backed by the U.S. government. However, established companies usually have safer rated bonds, while start-ups are much riskier. But less creditworthy companies offer a higher interest rate. These high-risk, high-return bonds are also called junk bonds.

BOND FACTS

How much interest bonds are offering is directly connected to the prevailing interest rates. Bonds, in fact, usually move inversely to interest rates. Why? Let's say you have a bond paying 5 percent. If interest rates move up to 6 percent, your bond pays less—that is, 5 percent—relative to new bonds, so it is worth less on the secondary market. The secondary market is where you go to find buyers if you want to sell your bond before its date of maturity. So rising interest rates may depress bond prices, and falling interest rates tend to boost bond prices.

Although you receive the full face value of the bond when it matures, its market value changes daily. As interest rates move up or down, the market readjusts bond prices to reflect the changes. If you do not plan to hold the bond to maturity, or if you invest in a bond mutual fund—as many individuals investing in bonds do—it's important to understand that bond prices (and bond fund share prices) change frequently.

And this presents another way in which to make money with bonds—through the secondary market. This simply means that you can sell your bonds in the secondary market at a price higher than what you paid—in other words, a premium.

ECON 101: THE FED

Let's take a look at the overall financial market. The Federal Reserve, or the Fed, is our nation's bank. It was created in 1913 to stabilize the nation's financial systems. Today, all banks are part of the Federal Reserve system. It's a corporation, owned by banks who have purchased stock shares. The Fed is run by a board of governors appointed by the president. There is one chairman who holds a four-year term.

WALL STREET WISDOM: ***Before you invest in bonds, you can check out their ratings. These ratings, which range from As to Ds (just like school), give you an idea of the likelihood that you'll get your money paid back.***

Three major companies study bonds and give them ratings:

1. *Moody's Investors Service*
2. *Standard and Poor's Corporation*
3. *Fitch Investors Service*

In addition to using these ratings, you can evaluate bonds by looking at the prospectus. Check to see the amount of debt already issued by the company. Heavy debt may signal caution.

The Fed lends money to banks at an interest rate called the *discount* rate. Fed officials also regularly examine every bank's records to regulate loans and ensure that regulations are met. The Fed also regulates the money supply in the economy. We need the right balance of money so that we don't hit inflation or a recession.

Why is inflation so important? It reduces your purchasing power. Let's say you save your $5 a day for ten years. You'll end up with approximately $18,000 if you've kept the money in a jar in your closet. That's great. However, let's say you were saving for an $18,000 Honda. By the year 2003, that Honda may cost $23,000 because of inflation. You need to track inflation, because the point of investing is to beat it.

Inflation occurs when there's too much money in the system. If money is plentiful, but there aren't enough goods to buy, prices go up. Although inflation seems like a bad thing, debtors, or those who borrow money, do well. When you repay a loan in inflationary times, you're actually repaying less than what you borrowed, since the money you're using to repay the loan isn't worth what it was when you borrowed it.

The Fed takes damaged currency and bills out of circulation and replaces them with new ones. The Fed also is a keeper of gold, right in New York at the New York Federal Reserve Bank. It's a massive underground vault that contains the largest known reserve of gold anywhere. Most of it, however, belongs to foreign nations, who count on the Fed's security.

MEASURING UP

Economists, investors, bankers, and analysts anxiously watch the economy to see how it's doing, and to guess how the stock market will do. You'll often hear the market referred to either as a *bull* market or a *bear* market. No one really seems to know how these names evolved. Some say that a bull thrusts upward while attacked, thus a bull market is a strong one, or one that's expected to rise. A bear paws downward; hence a bear market is one in decline, with declining prices.

So, how do experts judge the market? Interest rates are one way to track what's happening. For example, when there's a lot of money around, banks will offer low interest rates to entice people to borrow money. If there's less money around, banks will raise interest rates.

The twelve leading indicators are another way that experts judge the market. Pinpointed by government economists to gauge the future of the economy, these indicators include everything from stock prices to the number of unemployment claims made, to the average number of hours clocked by factory workers each week. Together, they help predict a possible recession or inflationary period.

A third way to observe the economy is the consumer price index, which is compiled by the Bureau of Labor Statistics. The CPI helps the government monitor inflation. Basically, it's the government calculation of cost-of-living expenses, such as housing, clothing, food, and transportation and health care.

INDEXES

Stock indexes are a way to help individual investors—and economists, stockbrokers, and money managers—judge how their investments are doing. Indexes help investors compare how their stocks or mutual funds are doing compared to others, or the general market. Stock indexes also help investors see which way stock prices are heading.

The Dow, for example, is a phrase that you probably hear a lot. It's short for the Dow-Jones industrial average—and it's perhaps the most famous stock index. It was invented by Charles Henry Dow, the first editor of the *Wall Street Journal.* The Dow averages the prices of thirty of the most popular stocks on the New York Stock Exchange. If the Dow goes up, generally it's good news for investors, because it reflects a general trend upward. If it goes down, investors may begin to fret.

Dow Jones & Co., who also publishes the *Wall Street Journal,* actually compiles four stock market averages: the industrial average, which consists of industrial stocks: the transportation average, comprised of transportation stocks; the utilities average, comprised of utility stocks, and a composite of sixty-five various stocks.

The Dow-Jones industrial average is still the standard most commonly used, although some claim that thirty stocks, especially since they are the stocks of older and established companies, cannot accurately reflect the entire market. The Dow stocks are chosen by a committee, and they do try to reflect the overall market. For example, when the country was dominated by industry, steel and other mills were represented. Today, technology and communications make a strong showing. The list is constantly changing, although some companies have been in its since its inception. The following are the companies that make up the 1998 Dow-Jones industrial average:

Alliedsignal
Aluminum Co. of America
American Express
AT & T
Boeing
Caterpillar
Chevron
Coca-Cola
Disney
Du Pont, E.I.
Eastman Kodak
Exxon Corporation
General Electric
General Motors
Goodyear Tire
Hewlett-Packard
International Business Machines (IBM)
International Paper
Johnson & Johnson
McDonald's Corp.
Merck & Co.
Minnesota Mining & Manufacturing
J. P. Morgan
Philip Morris Co.
Proctor & Gamble
Sears Roebuck and Co.
Travelers
Union Carbide
United Technologies
Walmart

WALL STREET WISDOM: ***According to financial history, stocks have never lost money over a twenty-year period. However, you have a one in three chance of losing money in the stock market if you invest for just one year, and a one in five chance of losing money if you invest for five years.***

Obviously, this is why you want to keep your short-term investment money out of the stock market: The risk may be too great. Any financial goal over three years, however, is fair game.

RISK

For most investors, a mix of investments, including cash or cash equivalents such as CDs or money market funds, stocks, and bonds, is the way to a balanced portfolio. Portfolio is merely the name given to the collection of assets—or investments.

The reason that you want a balance is to mitigate risk, which is always a part of investing on Wall Street. Whatever investment you choose, you are speculating. You are speculating whether a company will do well. You are speculating whether a town—or government—will be able to pay back a loan.

In addition to creating a balanced portfolio, or diversifying, there are other ways to reduce risk. One is by educating yourself. If you understand what the risks are of each investment type, you'll make wiser decisions. You can also use investment strategies to reduce your risk, such as dollar-cost averaging, where you contribute the same amount every month regardless of market conditions. Keep in mind, however, that the greatest risk of all may be taking too little risk.

WALL STREET WISDOM: *Here's a quick rundown of the risk you take with the different investment vehicles. Clip and save if you like. Here's another one of those quick n' sassy investment sayings—it's called the sleep rule of investing. Simply put, if you can't sleep at night, it's the wrong investment for you. Also, remember, the higher the reward, the greater the risk.*

Insomniacs' Guide to Investing: Futures

Commodities
Options
Gold
Junk bonds

Tossing and Turning: Corporate Bonds

Blue-chip stocks
Convertible bonds
Convertible bond funds (no fixed maturity date, so riskier)
Small-cap growth funds
Small-cap stocks

Resting Comfortably: Mutual Funds

Lots of REM States: U.S. Federal Agency Bond Funds

U.S. government securities, including bills, notes, and bonds
Money market mutual funds
Savings bonds

Sleeping like a Baby: Treasury Bills

U.S. government securities money funds
Federally insured bank accounts
Certificates of deposit
Savings accounts

If you play it too safe, you may also end up losing money—through inflation, or loss of purchasing power.

WALL STREET LINGO

You'll find a glossary at the back of this book. However, here, instead of the checklists you'll find at the end of other chapters, we're going to highlight some common Wall Street words and phrases that will help you, as you begin your investment journey.

Asset: Something that you own—a possession—that has value to you now and in the future. The three asset classes are known as stocks, bonds, and cash.

Asset Allocation: A fancy phrase that simply means how you invest your money, or how your assets are divvied up. A conservative asset allocation, for example, may be 30 percent in stocks, 40 percent in bonds, and 30 percent in fixed-income investments, or cash. Your asset allocation changes as your financial goals do.

Blue-chip Stocks: In poker, blue chips normally have the highest value. On Wall Street, a blue-chip stock is from a company that has a successful track record. Usually these companies are at the top of their industry, with high credit ratings. Of course, this is a subjective term, and a relative one. So while blue chip implies quality, it does not guarantee stability.

Correction: This is a euphemism for a downturn in the market, usually of at least 10 percent. There is some validity to the word "correction," however. The stock market, by its nature, goes up and down. Too much of a good thing can lead to stocks that are considered too expensive and too risky.

Diversification: This is similar, but not to be confused with, asset allocation. While asset allocation is how you spread your money over the different classes—stocks, bonds, and cash—diversification is varying your investments *within* these asset classes. For example, you are diversified when you buy different types of stocks within the stock portion of your portfolio.

Dollar-cost Averaging: This is the antithesis of timing the market, or trying to buy low and sell high. Although buying low and selling high is what most investors would prefer to do, dollar-cost averaging, or investing a set amount of money at set intervals regardless of the market, has actually been proven to be an effective investing tool. The underlying principle of dollar-cost averaging is that your money will, over time, buy more shares at the low prices than at the high prices.

Equities: Another name for stocks. When you buy a stock, you are buying equity in the company.

Inflation: Inflation is caused when the money supply grows too rapidly—in other words, when there's too much money to spend and not enough goods to spend it on. Therefore, consumer good prices go up. When you're trying to beat inflation, this means that you're trying to invest your money so you can beat the rate of inflation, historically 3 percent per year, so that you don't lose your purchasing power.

Mutual Funds: Developed in 1924, mutual funds are a collection of stocks, bonds, or other securities purchased by a group of investors and managed by a professional management company. Instead of buying individual stocks or bonds, investors pool their money and invest it together. The investment decisions are made by the mutual fund manager. Mutual funds are getting more and more specialized; this means that they serve specific investment objectives, such as growth, income, or safety.

Portfolio: The name for your overall investment picture.

Your investment portfolio should contain a mix of different investments, including stocks, bonds, and cash investments.

Risk: Every investment involves risk; it just depends on what type. There is the risk of losing money, or the decreasing value of your investment. There is also the risk of not risking enough, and losing out to inflation.

Total Return: Probably the best-known way of making money through stocks is through appreciation, or buying a stock at a low price and selling it at a high price. However, the point of investing is to make money, and there are different ways to do this. You can make money through appreciation, through income paid out by the stocks, and through tax savings. The total return is the overall picture of profit, and it's an important consideration when buying an investment.

FOUR

Retirement Plans: The Best Way to Start Investing $5 a Day

All my available funds are completely tied up in ready cash.
—W. C. Fields

WALL STREET NAVIGATOR: Finding your way around chapter 4

- Why retirement plans are the best place to start investing for the $5-a-day investor
- The benefits of tax-advantaged investment plans
- The ins and outs of retirement plans, including 401(k)s, IRAs, and Keoghs
- How to set up retirement accounts
- What investments to place in a retirement account
- The lexicon of retirement plans

For many people, a secure retirement is their primary investment goal. However, taking your first foray into investing by placing money into an account that you can't touch for years may not be your idea of excitement. But if you want thrills, ride a roller coaster.

Inaccessibility is part of what makes retirement plans such

great long-term investments. You can't touch the money until age fifty-nine and a half unless you want the Internal Revenue Service to penalize you (with a few exceptions that you'll hear about in a minute). And the last thing you want is to give extra money to the IRS. This means that you are forced to take advantage of compound interest and long-term investing in the stock market. Also, these plans have tax advantages, which means less money to the government and more money to you.

Besides, it's a good idea to think of your future. It's one of those abstract quantities that becomes concrete before you know it. As Americans, we're pretty up front about our lack of vision. And pretty muddled about it, too. A 1995 Kemper Roper-Starch survey said 65 percent of baby boomers acknowledge they're not saving enough for retirement, yet 68 percent believe they'll have enough to live on. That's a nice fairy tale!

Unfortunately, one follows the other. A retirement that leaves you with options and the freedom to live as you please—which is what security is all about—is not very likely to materialize unless you implement those characteristics we talked about in chapter one: commitment, discipline, and patience.

WHAT'S SO GOOD ABOUT RETIREMENT PLANS?

Most retirement plans are equipped with one of the best investing aids ever: The money that you use to invest is pretax money—or tax-deductible—and the money that you earn on your investments is tax-deferred.

A tax-deductible investment is one where the money that you deposit into a retirement account isn't taxed at the time you put it in. In other words, when it comes time to pay your taxes, you deduct from your yearly gross income the amount that you invest. Let's say that you deposit $5 a day—or approximately $1,800 a year—into a 401(k) or tax-deductible IRA. Let's also assume that you are in the 28 percent tax bracket. You will not be paying taxes on that $1,800, so that means you will save an additional $500 or so. Retirement plans are also tax-deferred, which means that what you earn in the account will not be taxed until you withdraw it. Take a look.

	Retirement account investing	**Non-retirement account**
$5 a day investment	$1,800	$1,800
Taxes on the money invested	0	$500
Subtotal	$1,800	$1,300
Historic 10% stock market return on your investment	$180	$130
Taxes on your investment earnings	0	$30
Total in one year	$1,980	$1,400

Of course, you will eventually pay taxes on the money when you withdraw it after age fifty-nine and a half, but the money will have grown tax-deferred over those years. If you are in a lower tax bracket at that time (which many people will be), the money that you'll earn through not paying taxes on that money (it makes your investment account grow that much faster) will be greater than the amount that you'll have to pay when you withdraw the money.

GETTING YOUR EMPLOYER TO PAY

Some retirement plans—employer-sponsored plans such as 401(k)s—possess another big advantage: Your contribution, or the money that you are putting in for yourself, is matched by your employer. In other words, your employer is giving you free money. Now what can be better than that?

Think about the time that you spend angling for raises or bonuses, or even negotiating a salary when you first take a job. Here, even on $5 a day, you may have a chance of adding 2, 3, even 5 percent of your salary just by saving for your future. And you don't have to earn this. If it's in your company's policy, they have to do it.

WALL STREET WISDOM: ***Although this may sound obvious, always try to invest in an employer-matching retirement plan before you make any other Wall Street investments. Simply put, you'll have a hard time matching the return that those employer contributions offer.***

SO GET GOING

What are the drawbacks to investing your $5 a day in a retirement account? Simple. These accounts are for retirement; therefore, this is long-time investing. This means sacrifice. And it also means patience, commitment, and discipline.

One of the best things about retirement plans is that you can get started on small amounts. In fact, most retirement plans *encourage* you to. That's the real beauty of this whole deal.

So take another look at your time line and goals. How much of your $5 a day can you afford to place into a retirement account and still be able to meet your shorter-term goals? For those goals, you'll want to invest in a savings account, CD, mutual fund, or more accessible account. But, again, the best place to start your investing is with your future.

What you'll find in this chapter is a rundown of your retirement plan options. You need to see which you qualify for, and which you think is best for you. You'll also find tips on managing these accounts, and places to go to open them up.

WALL STREET WISDOM: ***Wherever you decide to place your $5 a day, certain universal truths apply. We thought it might help to translate these truths into familiar sayings. Clichés work when they mean something to you.***

1. **A penny saved is a penny earned.** *A penny saved is really more than a penny earned, when you consider your tax savings. The first step to any intelligent investment plan is to realize that your money is finite, and that you can do a lot with a little.*
2. **Look before you leap.** *Consider your goals before you invest. And always do your homework. A hot tip is fine—if you check it out yourself before acting on it.*
3. **Don't put all your eggs in one basket.** *Always diversify your investments. If you place all your money in one investment—or even in several different investments in one asset class—you may hit a snag when the market fluctuates (and it will). Instead, spread your investment money over the different asset classes—stocks, bonds, and cash instruments.*
4. **Slow and steady wins the race.** *Some of the most effective investors have started out with little, invested consistently, and practiced patience. And although this is not about winning, it is about formulating an investment strategy that gives you the freedom to live your life. And that's winning.*

WHY EVEN THINK ABOUT RETIREMENT?

Many of you, especially those in their twenties and thirties, may find it hard to sock away money that you won't even see for another thirty or forty years. Perhaps your motto is live for today—to grab the gusto, and let tomorrow take care of itself.

After all, you just may win that lottery, inherit a windfall, marry well, or get a huge promotion. And you know what? You just might. But you might not, either. It never hurts to prepare for the future and let the rest of the chips fall where they may.

We'll let you in on a little secret: Your future is going to happen no matter how far off it seems. And when that future happens, you're going to need to be prepared. This is true perhaps more now than ever before, because the traditional job structures, federal programs, and economy are going under revolutionary changes.

CHANGES IN HOW AMERICA RETIRES

You may say that your parents and grandparents did all right on their own. They didn't know how to invest, and yet they spent their retirement traveling and buying presents for grandchildren. Why should you worry?

Well, for one thing, life expectancy rates have soared. A child born near the millennium has a life expectancy of 100. And while that's a good thing, it also means that there are more retirement years to finance. Age 65 will soon be more middle than old age. So think of this less as retirement money and more as a ticket to freedom—the freedom to pursue a new career, return to school, or take up an avocation.

In addition to the fact that we're living longer and expecting a higher quality from our retirement years is the push toward self-reliancy in retirement. In our ever-increasingly do-it-yourself society, the onus for retirement is falling on the individual's shoulders. More and more employers are relying on employees to make retirement plan decisions.

It used to be that most Americans stayed with one employer throughout their working years. This employer usually provided them with a pension. It was one of the perks of the

WALL STREET WISDOM: ***What's in a name?***

As you probably know by now, simple concepts in personal finance are made more intimidating by confusing language. For example, the words you'll hear over and over again in reference to retirement plans are defined-benefit *plans,* self-directed *plans, and* salary-reduction *plans. Here's an easy guide to cut back on confusion.*

Defined-benefit plans: *These are the traditional pension plans. They are called defined benefit because your benefits are set—you get a defined amount when you retire.*

Self-directed retirement plans: *These are the newer players, the 401(k)s, the 403(b)s, the IRAs. Simply put, you decide where to invest your money, and how much you'll put in per year (with limits, of course). Since these are often invested in the stock market, under your direction, you may not have a set idea of how much money you'll end up with. However, common sense plays into this. You can look at the historic returns of the different investment vehicles, and you can also transfer your money from stocks into fixed-income investments the closer you get to retirement.*

Salary-reduction plans: *These are 401(k)s or 403(b)s, or any type of retirement plan where your investment comes out of your salary before you pay taxes—hence the name.*

job. You didn't have to make any investment decisions. The company did that.

Most defined-benefit plans, as these are called, are what most of us think of as retirement plans. You have few options about how the money is invested. When you retire, you receive a regular monthly benefit over the course of the rest of your life. When you retire, in other words, you still draw a salary—typically 30 to 50 percent of what you were earning when you retired. Nothing is mandated by law; it's up to your employer.

Often, these pensions have cost-of-living increases built in. And sometimes your survivors receive a final payment. Or you can choose to take your money in a lump sum when you retire, and invest it as you want.

However, many companies are changing to self-directed retirement plans (we'll talk about them soon), which leave you to make the investment decisions, including the decision to invest no money at all! And because so many of us lack the knowledge to know what we're turning down, we say no to 401(k)s and 403(b)s (what these plans are called) when they are often the very best game in town for financial stability.

SOCIAL SECURITY MYTHS AND REALITIES

One reason that you want to take advantage of retirement plan investing is the instability of Social Security. When President Roosevelt introduced the Social Security Act in 1935, it was part of his New Deal, a recovery plan for the Great Depression. His plan, for the most part, is still in effect—Social Security encompasses disability payments, unemployment insurance, and retirement income plans. (He also recommended universal health care insurance.) Therefore, the retired are not the only recipients of Social Security; others are disabled workers and survivors of deceased workers. These are services from which we all benefit, and to which we all contribute.

If you remember from chapter 1, you pay for these services through the Federal Insurance Contribution Act (FICA). This money goes directly from your employer to the IRS. You'll see its deduction on your pay stub—the amount you pay is relative to your salary. Your employer matches your contributions. If you're self-employed, you pay both halves.

WALL STREET WISDOM: ***Do you want to know how much you'll receive from Social Security when you retire? Call the Social Security Administration (SSA) at 800-772-1213. Ask for the Request for Earnings and Benefit Estimate Statement. If you complete and return the form to the SSA, they will calculate how much money you've already paid into Social Security, and what benefits you can expect to receive.***

Once as reliable as a pension, Social Security has now become unreliable for several reasons. First, as we mentioned, life expectancy is increasing; therefore each American worker will need more money for retirement. Back in 1935, the average American lived to age sixty-five. Today, the average life expectancy is closer to eighty-five, and a child born near the millennium may live to age one hundred. Second, our population is aging. Today five workers work to support every retiree. This means that five Americans are contributing to Social Security through FICA for every one retiree. By the year 2030, the ratio will be two to one.

Also, Social Security payments for retirement are not mandated by law. Congress can always revoke this privilege. That's unlikely, but some reform in the system will have to take place if it is to remain solvent. What's probably going to happen is that you will receive lower payments, and be eligible to collect them at an older age.

WALL STREET WISDOM: ***The X-Files?***

According to Luntz Research Co., which surveyed five hundred 18 to 34 year olds—also known as Generation Xers—more young people believe in UFOs than in Social Security's existing by the time they retire.

WHAT ARE RETIREMENT PLANS, AND HOW DO YOU SIGN UP FOR THEM?

Several types of retirement plans exist. First we'll describe the players, and then list the best places to go to sign up for these accounts. Also, we'll give you safeguards to help protect yourself from the risks involved.

401(k) Plans

Also known as employer-assisted plans, or salary-reduction plans, 401(k) plans are retirement plans offered by your employer, and so you are eligible only if your employer offers one. Why are these called 401(k)s? Simply because 401(k) is the part of the tax code that allowed these to come into existence.

Ted Benna, a Philadelphia benefits consultant, helped create 401(k)s back in 1981 when he noticed that section 401(k) in America's pension law allowed this type of retirement program. Before 1981, most companies offered opportunities for employees to contribute money to their pensions after the money was already taxed. Benna saw that the 401(k) code would allow pre-tax dollars as well.

These accounts are tax-deferred and tax-deductible—and in many cases employers will match part of your contribution. Often these matching contributions are up to 50 percent of your contributions. Imagine what would happen if your local department store offered a 50 percent rebate on everything that you bought. Most of us would fall all over ourselves to get there. And yet many, many American employees still reject one of the best investing devices around with such objections as "I can't afford to," "I'll do it later," or "They're too complicated. I don't know what to invest in." Sound familiar?

It's much better to save the energy you would spend making excuses, and just do it. Here's the scoop.

As we mentioned above, in the past, the typical employer took care of the typical employee with a pension plan. Employees didn't know how the plans were invested, but they knew that they would receive money with which to live when they retired. These *defined-benefit plans* paid retirees a fixed monthly amount, or an annuity.

With 401(k)s, or *employee-directed plans,* you only receive what you put in, with interest of course. It's all up to you. So if you feel as though you have no extra cash to contribute to a 401(k), or you keep putting off getting started, you can actually harm yourself and your future quite a bit. And although employers are educating their employees more and more about these plans, too few people listen.

Lend me your ears.

WALL STREET WISDOM: ***As many as 15 to 25 percent of retirees are being shortchanged by their employers' defined-benefit plans.***

Most of these errors are due to complexity, such as using the wrong interest rates for calculations of lump sum distributions. Help yourself out as much as possible: Keep track of how they calculated your benefits, your length of service, and your highest earning years. If you're still working, ask for one benefit statement a year for your record keeping. (You're entitled to this by law.)

If you think there's been an error, the National Center for Retirement Benefits (800-666-1000) will research your situation for free. But they'll also keep 30 percent of any amount recovered.

401(k) Facts

401(k)s, although sponsored by your employer, are most likely not *run* by your employer. Most companies hire outside firms—usually a mutual fund company, a bank, or employee benefits consulting firm—to oversee their 401(k) plans. They charge your company fees, which are passed on to you.

When you join, you tell your employer how much (what percentage) of your income you would like to contribute. You then get to choose what investments you would like your money to go into. The money is deducted directly from your paycheck, so you are not likely to miss it. Since your contribution lowers your reported salary, you pay less taxes. (This is the tax-deductible part.)

When 401(k)s first began, you had very limited investment choices. You still have limited options, but they're increasing. The average employer now offers six choices, and some plans offer dozens. You can choose everything from mutual funds to fixed-income investments to company stock. Typically, you also have the right to change your portfolio allocation—or your investment choices—several times a year. And often, your employer will match your contributions, usually 50 cents for every dollar you put in.

The rise of 401(k)s, or self-directed plans, has meant the demise of employer-directed plans. This means more freedom for you—and more responsibility.

Investment Limits: You have a limit to what you can contribute to your 401(k). Right now this limit is $10,000 per year, but this figure is adjusted annually for inflation.

Investment Options: Nearly every 401(k) plan offers participants three ways in which the money can be invested. The first way is in stocks, or stock mutual funds. The second is in bonds, or bond mutual funds, and the third is money market instruments, or fixed-rate investments. You have the option of switching your money from investment to investment at different set times.

Investment Time Frame: When you deposit money in a 401(k), you're putting it in there for the long term. That means you can't take it out without sacrificing 10 percent of it through penalty fees.

There are exceptions; called hardship withdrawals. If you die, your family can access the money. If you become disabled, you can access the money. If you are fifty-five years old and are separated from your job for any reason at all, you can take the money out without penalty. Also, if the 401(k) is part of a divorce settlement, it can be accessed early without penalty.

What happens, you may be asking, if you decide to change jobs?

You're not penalized if you take the money and place it in another retirement plan, but it has to go directly from the old plan into the new. Under no circumstances should you take the money yourself, even though, by law, you have 60 days to roll it over into another account.

Why? Because if you receive it directly, the IRS requires your employer to treat it as a distribution—or early withdrawal. You'll see 20 percent deducted from your money for taxes. Now, if you reinvest the money into another account within the specified period, you'll get that 20 percent back as a refund at tax time. But you'll have to come up with the missing 20 percent yourself until then. Otherwise, you'll have to pay taxes and early penalty charges—10 percent—on the 20 percent left behind.

Many, many people, however, make the mistake of taking that money when they leave a job as bonus money. That's a huge investing mistake. Not only do you lose the momentum of the compound interest but you also lose the 10 percent through penalties. AND you'll get taxed on the amount as well—to the tune of 20 percent of the whole. So you're looking at a loss of approximately 30 percent.

When you turn fifty-nine and a half, you can withdraw money (it's now taxable income) or roll it into an individual retirement account or an annuity. You must, however, begin to withdraw the money by age seventy and a half if you are retired. Folks at age seventy and a half who are not yet retired have the option of deferring withdrawals until they actually retire.

Protection: Don't worry, your employer may bag out on you, but they can't touch your 401(k). It's protected from creditors if your employer should declare bankruptcy. If you die, your 401(k) is an inheritable asset. It can be continued on a tax-deferred basis by spouse or child.

WALL STREET WISDOM: ***Like all retirement plans, 401(k)s are for the long term. Since we are a country of job-hoppers and short-term investors, remember to continue to treat your 401(k) as a retirement plan when you switch jobs. Here, in a nutshell, is what to do with your 401(k) when you make a career move.***

1. *First of all, do not take the distribution directly. If you do, the IRS will treat this as early withdrawal and charge you 10 percent penalty, plus approximately 20 percent in taxes.*
2. *Instead, to avoid taxes and penalties, arrange for the plan to go directly from your old custodian to your new one. Check with your old—and new—Human Relations Departments. (You can also keep your 401(k) intact, with your old employer, although some have minimum requirements.)*
3. *Your best bet, however, may be to roll over your money from your old employer's 401(k) into an Individual Retirement Account (IRA). With an IRA, you have a much wider range of investment choices, and more control over your investment. As with any IRA, you first need to find a custodian—a bank, mutual fund company, or discount broker that offers Individual Retirement Accounts. Usually, your new custodian will arrange for your money to go directly from your old plan into your new.*

Key: Start contributing as soon as possible, and as much as possible. You won't regret it. Just think, if you invested your $5 a day in a 401(k), you might end up actually investing closer to $8 a day through employer contributions and tax savings.

Investment Allocation: You're in it for the long term, so you want to think of long-term growth. One of the greatest mistakes that most beginning, investors make is that they play it too safe with their long-term investments. If you have

WALL STREET WISDOM: ***Here's a rundown on some of the more common investments offered in 401(k) plans.***

Balanced funds: *Similar to asset allocation or lifestyle funds, these funds offer you a diversified, or balanced, investment within one fund, usually a mix of stocks, bonds, and cash.*

Stock index funds: *Also known as equity income funds, these are a mix of stocks that approximate one of the major stock indices—usually the S & P 500.*

Since these funds reflect the market, they don't offer you the potential to outperform it. However, interestingly enough, they often outperform other stock funds.

Stock funds: *As the name suggests, these are funds that specialize in equities or stocks. Some of the common categories include* ***aggressive growth funds,*** *which usually invest in the stock of small, start-up companies. These stocks have the potential to outperform other kinds—as much as by 2 percent over the long-term—but they are risky as well.* ***Emerging market funds*** *are another risky investment. These are the stocks of companies outside the U.S.* ***Sector funds*** *invest in one specific area of the market—technology, for example, or real estate. The performance of these funds is directly related to how well that specific part of the market is doing.*

Company stock: *This is, simply, the stock of the company for which you work. Even though your company may be in great shape, it's a risky investment. Why? Because you already rely on your company for your paycheck and your benefits. Relying on them for your retirement money is a bit like putting all your eggs in one basket.*

Some companies offer nothing but company stock in their 401(k) plans. And others make company contributions contingent on your choosing company stock.

a long-term investment horizon, it's usually a good idea to invest in the stock market, where the average historic return is 10 percent. If you stick with guaranteed investment contracts (GIC), you might not beat inflation. You always want to balance safety with risk. See the Ask a Financial Planner section at the end of this chapter.

Liquidity: As you now know, the drawback to these accounts is that, basically, they're forced savings. You can't withdraw the money unless you can either prove a hardship or leave your job. What are your options, then, if you need the money before you hit age fifty-nine and a half?

You can borrow against your account if your plan allows this—some don't. Usually, you can borrow up to 50 percent of what is vested. In most plans, you are fully vested (which means you are eligible for your employer's contributions, too) after five years in an account. If you borrow from your account, you set up a pay-back schedule, complete with interest payments.

Since your interest payments go back into your account, it's not a bad place to look for a loan. However, if you default on the loan and do not pay back accordingly to terms, it's as if you withdrew your money early. You will be subject to penalties and taxes. And, if you change jobs, you may have to pay back the loan immediately or face penalties and taxes.

You can also withdraw the money if you can prove that you have no other reasonable means—including savings accounts, stocks, mutual funds, bonds, a house—for emergency funds, which include buying a house, avoiding eviction, paying tuition or a doctor's bill. Even though this is allowed, you are still subject to a 10 percent early withdrawal penalty and regular income tax. You can also begin to withdraw the money without penalty before you hit fifty-nine and a half, if you take the money in at least five equal annual installments until you hit age fifty-nine and a half.

WALL STREET WISDOM: ***It wasn't until 1996 that 401(k) participants put more money into stocks than guaranteed investment contracts, which, as their name suggests, deliver a fixed annual return.***

This can be dangerous, because you may get beat by inflation this way. Try to keep a balance of risk and safety in your retirement portfolio. The further you are from retirement, the more risk you can afford to take.

Fees and Other Costs. Mutual funds are required by law to disclose their fees, but 401(k)s are not. Part of the reason is the fact that the law that governs retirement plans, The Employee Retirement Income Security Act (ERISA), was actually written in 1974, seven years before the first 401(k).

Mutual fund companies oversee the largest percentage of 401(k)s, over 30 percent. Next in line is insurance companies, which oversee just under 30 percent. Banks 24 percent, and 14 percent in-house managers administer.

It is your employer's job to make sure that the 401(k) fees are reasonable. However, many employers know little about retirement plans. This is especially true for small or midsize plans. Therefore, you should educate yourself about costs. If your plan's fees seem high, see if you can convince your employer to minimize fees.

401(k) fees are rarely justified. A portion of the fees goes toward administrative costs, but a majority—over 80 percent—is usually just for investment services, a negligible concept at best. Although it is claimed that your fees depend on size and service, they are in fact arbitrary. Often plans charge a lot because they can—because of ignorance. If you work for a smaller firm, chances are you may be paying higher 401(k) fees. Why? Because your plan will have fewer assets, therefore less profit for the company, and you may have a less skilled negotiator at the helm.

Most investors in 401(k) plans do not even know the fees that they are paying. Check it out.

WALL STREET WISDOM: ***Retirement plans are part of the bigger picture.***

Your retirement investing is just one part of your whole portfolio. That means that you should coordinate your efforts within retirement plans with your efforts outside of the plans.

For example, if your portfolio goal is to have 70 percent stocks, 20 percent bonds, and 10 percent cash investments, your retirement plan should reflect this allocation.

Salary Reduction Plans for Nonprofit Organizations—or 403(b)s

403(b)s differ just slightly from 401(k)s. How?

Well, for one thing, 403(b)s are for employees of nonprofit organizations, such as hospitals, colleges, and universities. Rules for contributions, rollovers, and early withdrawals are nearly the same as for 401(k) plans.

Typically, however, your investment choices are even more limited than they are with 401(k) plans. When 403(b)s were created, they were created as tax-sheltered annuities. Which almost always come with extra fees—mortality and expense charges—that can eat more than 1.3 percent of the account value per year. However, Congress has added the option of placing tax-sheltered 403(b) money into mutual

WALL STREET WISDOM: *It helps if you have numbers on hand for 401(k) support:*

The 401(k) Association: *800-320-401K*
This group offers general advice on 401(k)s. Headed by Ted Benna himself.

401(k) Forum: *415-778-0600. http://www.401kforum.com*
If you're comfortable on-line, this Internet-based service can help you manage your 401(k).

Employee Benefit Research Institute: *202-659-0670*
This gives you background on the various benefit programs offered through the workplace.

The U.S. Department of Labor: *202-219-6666*
Always good to have this number handy. They can help if you find discrepancies in your plan or disagree with your plan managers.

funds. Therefore, you are allowed to invest in stock funds inside these plans.

Individual Retirement Accounts (IRAs)

IRAs were started in 1981 by the federal government to entice the average American to save for his or her retirement. The government wanted to decrease the number of seniors relying on the government for subsistence. These IRAs, now referred to as traditional IRAs, were supplemented by Roth IRAs with the 1997 Taxpayer Relief Act. We'll talk about the Roth IRA in a minute: First, the traditional IRA. Everyone who earns money is eligible for a traditional IRA; however, how much is tax-deductible depends on your income level

WALL STREET WISDOM: ***Here's a question for you: What's the difference between tax-deductible and tax-deferred?***

If an investment is tax-deductible, that means you don't pay taxes on it. Savvy? Let's take a hypothetical investor: Jonathan. He earns $30,000 as a sales rep. He's in the 28 percent tax bracket, which means that 28 percent of his salary—$8,000—goes to taxes. That's a lot of money. Now, if he invests in a tax-deductible investment, such as a mutual fund within an IRA, or a 401(k), he lessens the amount he has to pay in taxes. For example, if he invests $1,800 in an IRA, he pays taxes on a salary of only $28,200. That'll be a savings of approximately $500. Not a bad deal. Granted, you have to pay taxes when you withdraw the money, but you may be in a lower tax bracket.

If an investment is tax-deferred, that means you don't pay taxes on the interest—or money—that you are making from that investment. So Jonathan's immediate savings may be less, but, as you saw in the chart above, tax-deferred compound interest is a lovely thing.

and whether you have a 401(k) available to you through your work.

If you're covered by a pension or other retirement plan, such as a 401(k) at work, or earning more than $35,000 as a single person or more than $50,000 married, you're out of deduction luck—but not out of tax-deferral luck.

We know that tax-deductible plans are great; plain old tax-deferred status is not so bad either. A word of caution for those using IRAs for tax-deferral, but not tax-deductible, reasons: Keep good records proving that you paid tax on the money you invested. Otherwise Uncle Sam won't take your word for it and will charge you taxes again when you withdraw the money.

Why would you use a traditional IRA, when you have exposure to other retirement plans? One, you've maxed out your other plans. (Keep in mind that even if you max out your deductible contributions to a 401(k), 20 percent of employers allow you to make a nondeductible contribution to the plan.) Second, you swear you won't need that money until you're fifty-nine. And you're ready to really take advantage of long-term investing.

It's easy to open up an IRA. You need to contact the bank, insurance company, brokerage firm, or mutual fund company, and you fill out an application. The financial institution that you choose is called the custodian. But you are the one who decides what to do with the money. This is completely different from the traditional pension, where you had nearly no say in your investing, and even from 401(k)s and 403(b)s, where you have limited choices. With an IRA, you can choose to invest in a CD, a mutual fund, an individual stock through a Dividend Reinvestment Program, or even just a savings account.

In fact, you can invest in nearly anything with your IRA account. The only investments precluded by law include collectibles, such as stamps, paintings, or antiques; commodities; and investments made with borrowed money. That doesn't mean that you can't borrow money to invest in an IRA; it merely means you can't use margined stocks, commodity figures, or mortgaged real estate.

Everyone is limited to a maximum investment of $2,000 per year. Otherwise, the government figured, IRAs would give too great an advantage to the wealthy. And, as we said above, depending on how much money you make, and whether you have another retirement plan available to you at work, your contribution may or may not be tax-deductible.

Many people began using IRAs as an easy way to save—because of the tax deductions—rather than looking at them as true investment vehicles. But IRAs *are* investments, just like any others where you have to consider diversification, long-term growth and risk, and asset allocation. Of course, the closer you are to retirement, the less risk you want to take with your investments.

WALL STREET WISDOM: ***Because the great advantage to IRAs is the fact that they are tax-deferred—that is, you don't pay taxes on the money or its earnings until you withdraw it—it makes no sense to include investments that are already tax-deferred, such as municipal bonds, tax shelters, and deferred annuities.***

IRA Investment Limits: Kids can also open IRAs, but they have to have earned income. (Another enticement for that paper route.) They, too, have a $2,000 yearly limit. Now, that money doesn't necessarily have to come from their earned income. In other words, if they receive a gift of $2,000, and also earn $2,000, they can spend their income and use the gift money for their IRA.

You can open as many IRAs as you like, using a different custodian or investment each year. You still cannot contribute more than $2,000 per year, but this way you spread your risk.

Also, you can contribute all your money at once: you can put in that $2,000 windfall from your garage sale, for instance; or you can arrange for automatic deductions, say of $5 a day, or you can contribute nothing for any particular year. You can set up an account, place the minimum needed, and then forget about it, although we don't recommend that.

If you make deductible contributions, you have to pay taxes on both the money and the earnings when you withdraw the money. Obviously, if you make contributions that are taxed, you don't have to pay tax again on that money when you take it out. You'll only pay money on the interest that you earned.

Where Do I Get an IRA?: You can open an IRA nearly anywhere these days. With all these options, you can shop around. Make sure you consider expenses. These will directly affect your portfolio. Sometimes these fees are hidden. Don't be afraid to ask. If you do get charged an annual fee, pay it separately, so that it doesn't come out of your valuable IRA contribution.

One place to open an IRA is your local bank. Keep in mind that you'll most likely end up in savings vehicles for an investment, such as money market funds and CDs. Many banks now offer mutual funds, but bank mutual funds often have high fees, or loads. And you know what we think about these.

Good place to open an IRA is with a mutual fund company, especially if you can enter one with a minimum amount automatically deposited each month. We'll talk about this in the next chapter.

WALL STREET WISDOM: ***Guess what? The early bird does get the worm.***

You can make a lot more money if you make your IRA investments earlier in the year. Hard to believe, but true. Since we are a nation of procrastinators, most of us wait until the beginning of April to make our IRA contributions.

According to Scudder, Stevens & Clark, if you invest the maximum yearly amount into your IRA—$2,000—on January 1 of each year, the earliest you can contribute, rather than waiting until April 15 of the following year, the last date to contribute, you'll reap benefits.

Over a twenty-year period with a rate of return at 10 percent, you would earn $15,000 more.

Also, some discount brokers offer no-transaction-fee accounts, where you can build an IRA with multiple funds from different fund families. And if you want to mix and match, there's no transaction fee (hence the name).

Investment Time Frame: Again, when you invest in a retirement plan, such as an IRA, it's for the long term. If you withdraw the money before age fifty-nine and a half, the IRS will penalize you 10 percent. You'll also have to pay taxes on the money you withdraw. You can begin to withdraw your money from your IRA, like a 401(k), after age fifty-nine and a half, and you must take it out by age seventy and a half.

Although this may be hard to believe, some people inadvertently deposit over $2,000 per year into their IRAs. If you do this, take it out immediately, or you will be penalized at 6 percent annual tax. In addition, you may have to pay a 10 percent penalty when you withdraw the money.

Of course, if you withdraw the money early, before you hit fifty-nine and a half, you face a 10 percent penalty. And remember, you're not paying just the 10 percent penalty, you're also paying tax on the money that you withdraw. It counts as earnings.

Investment Allocation: As with any retirement plan, you always want to be aware of your time line. And the further you are from retirement, the more risk you can, and should, take. The greatest mistake you can make in an IRA is playing it too safe, or not diversifying your assets.

The Roth IRA: Some of the best news from the 1997 tax law comes in the form of the *back-loaded IRA,* also known as the Roth IRA, after William Roth (R-Del), its chief proponent in the Senate. Instead of the immediate tax breaks usually available through the traditional IRA, the Roth IRA gives tax breaks at the back end, when you withdraw the money.

WALL STREET WISDOM: ***What kind of asset mix is right for your 401(k) or IRA? Much depends on how far you are from retirement. The following breakdown should act as a guideline:***

Twenty years or more from retirement

45 percent U.S. stock
30 percent international stock
15 percent small company stock
10 percent emerging markets

Ten years to retirement

40 percent U.S. stock
15 percent international stock
5 percent emerging markets
30 percent fixed-income investments

Close to or in retirement

20 percent U.S. stock
10 percent international stock
5 percent emerging markets
60 percent fixed-income investments

This is how it works. Your after-tax money—still a $2,000 annual maximum—goes into the account, so contributions are not tax-deductible. However, you pay no taxes on the money when you withdraw it. You can't tap into the tax-free withdrawals until you're at least age fifty-nine and a half and the account has been open for at least five years. As with the other retirement accounts, if you take early withdrawals, you're subject to taxes and a 10 percent penalty. However, unlike the other plans, you can keep your money in Roth IRAs forever. You can convert your traditional IRA to a Roth but first you must pay tax on the old IRA in order to move the money.

When choosing between a traditional IRA and a Roth IRA, consider the following: If your tax rate will be higher when you withdraw the money than it is now, your choice is clear: You'll want to go for the Roth IRA. However, if you wind up in a lower tax bracket, you'll want to pay taxes later, with a traditional IRA. However, calculations of after-tax values are complex, and include variables such as your age, current and projected tax brackets, and income. If you have access to the Internet, check out the Strong Funds site at www.strongfunds.com or T. Rowe Price's www.troweprice.com for individualized help.

Starting in 1998, it is possible to tap an IRA early to buy a first home for yourself, your children, grandchildren, or parents. You can withdraw up to $10,000 without penalty; however, you will be taxed in your top tax bracket.

Retirement Plans for the Self-employed: Keogh Plans and SEP-IRAs

It's hard to be self-employed and hear all the wonderful news about 401(k)s. You may feel out of the loop. However, here are some retirement plans that level the playing field. Of course, as a self-employed person, you're eligible for the full $2,000 annual tax-deductible contribution to an Individual Retirement Account, or, of course, you can take advantage of a Roth IRA. If, one day, you want to exceed $5 a day investing, here's the good news: Whether you are the head of a business, or sell lemonade on the sidewalk, you can open your own retirement account that goes above and beyond an IRA. In fact, these retirement plans for the self-employed offer some of the same perks—they are tax-deferred and tax-deductible—but you can contribute much more than the $2,000 yearly IRA limit. (That would have to be some lemonade stand, but there you go.)

To qualify for an SEP or a Keogh plan, as they are called, you merely need to be self-employed—either part or full time. In other words, you have to fill out Form 1099 with the IRS at tax time.

SEP-IRAs (Simplified Employee Pension Plans): These retirement plans are for both small business and sole owners of businesses. SEPs allow contributions of approximately 13 percent of your self-employment income, not more than $22,500 annually. If you are also an employee of your own company, you can contribute up to 15 percent of your annual income, but not more than $30,000 annually. When you establish an SEP, simply open an IRA (any time before the filing deadline for the tax year in which your contributions will be claimed) at a bank, mutual fund company, or insurance company. Paperwork is minimal. You are still eligible to contribute $2,000 annually to your regular IRA.

Keoghs: Keoghs are more complicated than SEPs. For one thing, you must keep detailed records for the IRS *and* the Department of Labor, and Keoghs are difficult to set up. Also, there are several variations of Keoghs, including defined-benefit Keoghs, money-purchase Keoghs, and profit-sharing Keoghs. Your best bet is talking to an accountant about these. What are the advantages? You can set aside more money in a Keogh than in an SEP-IRA—up to 20 percent of your annual income, or up to $30,000 per year. You can also set up vesting schedules with Keoghs, which allow retirement money for employees, based on their years of service. Keoghs are best for larger companies where vesting is an issue. (If you establish a Keogh for yourself, you must extend its benefits to your employees.)

SIMPLE Plans: These are for the self-employed and companies with 100 or fewer employees. You can contribute up to $6,000 per year, all tax-deductible and tax-deferred. You will be faced with the same 10 percent IRS penalties for early

WALL STREET WISDOM: ***According to our Ask a Financial Planner, Darryl Reed, the following five mistakes are the most common—ones the small investor can make in retirement plans.***

1. ***Not educating yourself:*** *Ignorance is not bliss when it comes to managing your money. Get your information straight—even if you have to spend a little time or money on it. You'll end up paying one way or the other.*
2. ***Procrastinating:*** *Usually there's no good reason to put off investing other than procrastination. At the risk of sounding trite, just do it.*
3. ***Not setting specific goals with specific dollar amounts:*** *If you don't know why you're investing—or saving—it might just feel like one more restriction in your life. And you'll be less likely to follow through.*
4. ***Not having a target rate of return:*** *This makes a huge difference when it comes time to choose investment vehicles. Let's say that traveling around the world when you retire is a goal. And you've figured out you need to invest X amount of money for X number of months at a rate of return of 10 percent to reach this goal. It's not going to happen if you put your IRA money in a money market account.*
5. ***Not sticking with it:*** *At first, when you're investing with smaller amounts of money, you may not see the results. This causes some investors to grow discouraged. However, that money is accumulating, and it will pay off. And if you don't invest it, the same amount of time is still going to pass.*

withdrawal, and you must begin to withdraw your money by age seventy and a half. You can set these up in the same places where you can set up an IRA; the paperwork is a no-brainer.

ASK A FINANCIAL PLANNER

Darryl Reed speaks: Joe decided he is going to contribute 6 percent of his salary or $144 per month to his 401(k) plan. Since the newspaper where he works matches 50 cents on the dollar up to the first 6 percent of employee contribution, he will, in effect, be putting away $216 per month. This is an immediate return on his money. At this rate, he could have somewhere close to $500,000 for retirement at age fifty-five, assuming he invests largely in stocks or stock funds, and that he receives an average 10 percent rate of return.

Joe's mix of assets for his 401(k) should be aggressive. He understands that the stock market fluctuates. He also realizes that his retirement is twenty-nine years away. His allocation should be about 90 percent equity, or stocks, and 10 percent fixed-income. We're also taking into account his savings emergency reserve. He has projected that amount to be approximately $2,500. He has about $2,100 to go, since he has $400 in savings right now.

Investors should always look at their overall picture. Don't separate out your different investments, such as retirement plans, stock market investments, and savings accounts, but rather view these as part of a greater whole.

Joe's mix should look something like the following:

10 percent intermediate-term fixed-income assets
25 percent small-company funds
20 percent large company funds
10 percent medium-company funds
30 percent foreign stock funds
5 percent REITs

Joe should hold the fixed-income assets and large-company funds in the 401(k), depending on his choices in the plan. This way his taxable income distributions will be minimal.

• David should immediately start to contribute to his 403(b) plan at work. The power of compound interest is immense, and he really needs to put that to work for himself as quickly as possible. David and Tess should consider starting with $100 per month, which is only about 2.5 percent of their gross salary. They should increase that amount as much as possible in the near future after they have increased their emergency reserves.

Additionally, Tess should look into the possibility of being able to contribute to a retirement account through her employer. You always want to take advantage of tax-advantaged savings.

David and Tess both understand the long-term nature of stock market investments, although Tess is a bit more concerned about the daily ups and downs. Given all factors, an investment mix of 80 percent equities and 20 percent fixed-income seems appropriate. Most of their investing is for retirement, with a few short- and intermediate-term goals.

The mix of investments might be broken down as follows:

20 percent intermediate-term fixed-income assets
15 percent large cap growth
15 percent large cap value
10 percent small cap value
10 percent small cap growth
30 percent international equity

• When Carla is talking to her employer, Tom, about life insurance issues, it would also help if she had some information about the new SIMPLE retirement plans. It's doubtful that Tom would be willing to set up a 401(k) plan because of the annual administrative costs, but a SIMPLE plan may be just what he has been looking for. Although Luscious Landscaping would have to match 3 percent of whatever Carla decides to contribute, it is much more palatable than trying to set up a 401(k) plan.

Most 401(k) plans have an administrative cost of several thousand dollars associated with them. Not a good thing for any business, but especially unattractive to a small business. Besides, Tom has been looking at how he can save more for retirement, and some of the other employees have expressed an interest in some sort of plan. If all goes well, Carla should look into saving at least $50 per month.

Carla's number-one priority should be her retirement account. Even if she never becomes the homeowner she dreams of becoming, she needs to make sure she has enough food and shelter for her entire life.

An appropriate asset mix for retirement may be 60 percent stocks and 40 percent bonds, broken down as follows:

40 percent intermediate-term bond funds
25 percent large-company funds
15 percent small-company funds
20 percent international funds

• John should consider a traditional IRA to defer taxes on his earned income. Since Marge and John estimate that they may work about five years more, they can

WALL STREET REVISITED: Checklist for chapter 4

1. *If you are eligible for a 401(k) at work, enroll. It's a great way to take advantage of a tax-deferred and tax-deductible investing. Also, your employer may match part of your contributions.*
2. *If you're not eligible, open an IRA either traditional or Roth. You can have both, but your yearly contribution limit can never exceed 2,000—total. Watch the fees, and make sure you have a portfolio mix that matches your financial goals.*
3. *Even if you are eligible for a 401(k), still consider opening a Roth IRA. While your contributions may not be tax-deductible earnings grow tax-free.*
4. *Consider your retirement investing to be just that—for your retirement. Don't be tempted to withdraw the money early. You'll pay for it dearly.*

defer their taxes at least for a while. Over that five-year period, John may earn about $37,000 (fifty weeks per year, no raises taken into account). Even if he saves only 75 percent of that, it's a nest egg of $33,000 (estimated annual earnings of 8 percent). At age seventy, invested in a Treasury, it's enough to generate income of about $2,145 per year (at 6.5 percent interest). Not a lot of money, but certainly enough to allow John and Marge to eat out a few more times per month. And that's not touching the principal.

FIVE

Mutual Funds: The $5-a-Day Investor's Best Friend

Money is good for bribing yourself through the inconviences of life.
—Gottfried Reinhardt

OK, you're saying, retirement plans are all well and good, but you want to invest money so that you can get your hands on it in less than twenty years from now. You also want the chance to be without the restrictions of retirement plans' maximum contributions and transfer rules.

You're not sure how to invest directly in the stock market, though. Too much risk, you think. It's true. The big risk with stocks is that they can decrease in value. In any given year, the stock market can fluctuate. Another great risk you run into as an investor is not diversifying your portfolio enough. It takes a lot of time, energy, and money to monitor and diversify an effective investment portfolio.

So what's a viable way to enter the stock market on $5 a day? Mutual funds. Mutual fund companies won't match your contributions, nor do they offer the tax advantages, but they are a great place to put your $5 a day *after* you fund your retirement plan.

Mutual funds, which pool the money of many, many investors, offer inherent diversification. In addition, they are managed by professionals. So not only do you get a professional manager—someone who is paid to watch the trends and market conditions—but you also have the opportunity to own hundreds of stocks for only a few hundred dollars.

Mutual funds are also accessible; they're easy to get into and easy to get out of. You also have a variety of funds from which to choose. They are also relatively inexpensive and convenient. Perfect, in fact, for the $5-a-day investor. This chapter will provide you with the basics of mutual funds and the ways in which you can get started investing in them. You'll find the names of the top funds, resources, and discount brokers.

Happy investing.

WALL STREET WISDOM: ***You want to talk boom? In 1980, only 6 percent of American households were invested in mutual funds. In 1997, there were twice as many mutual funds on the market as there were stocks on the New York Stock Exchange, and over 30 percent of American households owned mutual funds.***

WHAT IS A MUTUAL FUND?

If you were to diversify your portfolio on your own, it would cost you a great deal of money because you would need to buy different stocks across a variety of industries or countries. Most experts recommend that you have approximately ten individual stocks in your portfolio to hedge against a market downturn. Mutual funds, however, offer an easy way to diversify your portfolio at a fraction of the cost.

Here's how they work: Let's say you and five friends get

together. You hire the neighborhood stock market whiz—let's call him Steve—as the manager of your little investment venture. You all pool your money and give it over to Steve. Steve, maybe for a few beers and pizza, does the research and makes the investment decisions.

You even decide on a theme for the portfolio—perhaps you all love Bob Dylan. Maybe you'll choose to invest in stocks and bonds that deal with Dylan, perhaps a recording company, a Minneapolis-based company, or guitar manufacturer.

Each member of this circle of friends has contributed money, so you all reap the benefits. And none of you has to do much work, because Steve monitors the stocks, chooses new ones, decides when to sell some of them. He, in short, tries to make sure the portfolio is balanced, profitable, and diversified.

That's the layman's view of mutual funds.

TECHNICAL STUFF

Now let's get technical. Mutual fund companies are actually corporations called investment companies whose sole purpose for being in business is to invest money for individuals—people like you. The first American mutual fund, the Massachusetts Investors Trust, was organized in 1924. But then the Great Depression hit, followed by World War II. Mutual funds nearly sputtered to a halt. Fewer than 100 existed by the late 1940s. From the 1960s onward, their numbers began to rise. Today over 8,000 exist, in every imaginable variety. The first mutual funds were invested only in stocks and corporate bonds. Now they include nearly every type of investment under the sun, including money markets, municipal bonds, and U.S. government bonds, to name just a few.

You can also find a fund for just about every interest. There are ''green funds'' for the environmentally aware. Technology buffs can invest in technology funds. You can even find funds that invest in stocks and bonds of a specific country. Even kids now have their own mutual funds. These usually invest in companies with kid appeal, such as Disney, The Gap, or Coca-Cola.

When you invest in a mutual fund, you become part of the action. You can help to elect the fund's board of directors. But don't worry, the investors are not the only ones monitoring the fund. Any mutual fund that does business over state lines is regulated by the SEC and must provide full disclosure to prospective shareholders in a *prospectus,* a published account of the who, what, and wheres of the fund. What they don't have to provide in the prospectus is a list of the fund's investments. You can get that in the fund's most recent quarterly or annual report. (You can also find this information in the Value Line and Morningstar publications, available at your public library.) If you know where a fund is invested—for example, Coca-Cola, Intel, Philip Morris—you get an idea of how diversified the fund is. It also gives you an idea of what type of fund it really is, since mutual fund names can be misleading.

All mutual funds operate the same way. They sell shares (that's how you enter a fund) to the public. That's you. They sell these shares at net asset value (NAV), which is the total assets of the fund—everything the fund owns—divided by the outstanding shares (how many shares are left to buy) minus the liabilities—what the fund owes.

Mutual funds invest in stocks, bonds, and cash instruments, such as money market securities, or even CDs. When you invest in a mutual fund, you are actually investing in the mutual fund company, but this particular company's assets are the stocks, bonds, and cash instruments that it owns. Your investment, which is the price of your shares, goes up or down with the value of the securities in which your fund has invested.

What's the catch? Nothing too major, just some caveats. One is that you often need a minimum amount to invest in mutual funds—sometimes around $2,500. However, many fund families allow you to invest with them for a reasonable minimum amount—sometimes as low as $50 a month, if you commit to investing regularly for a set period of time. Other funds just have low minimums, period. However, these funds often have higher loads.

LOADS, FEES, AND OTHER EXPENSES

Loads, our second caveat, are the commissions that mutual fund companies charge the investor for doing business with them. Most of the time, load funds are sold through brokers, agents, or financial planners who are licensed to sell these funds. The idea is that these brokers or agents are giving you advice; therefore they charge you a commission. But some load funds are sold directly from the mutual fund companies, who give you no advice on what to buy.

You should only buy funds from a commissioned agent or broker if you need advice on what funds to buy, or advice on asset allocation. In the same way, you should only buy a load fund directly from a mutual fund company if you really want that fund and are prepared to pay extra for it. Don't buy into the idea that load funds are better managed. No evidence exists to prove that load funds perform better than no-load funds. Your best bet is nearly always to go with the no-load funds. When you have only $5 a day to invest, you don't want a penny of that going to someone else.

How much are loads? They range from 3 percent to nearly 9 percent of the money that you invest. The average load is approximately 5 percent. That's a big bite from your investment. If you invest $1,000 in a mutual fund with a 5 percent load, only $950 of your money will actually be invested. Loads are sometimes tricky to spot. You will find front-end, back-end, and level loads. Look at the next Wall Street Wisdom box for a complete rundown.

WALL STREET WISDOM: ***The following load structures will help you know what to ask when you're buying a mutual fund:***

Remember, just because someone calls a fund a no-load fund doesn't necessarily mean it's so. This quick rundown will help you discern whether your money is going toward investment or toward a commission.

Front-end loads: *Front-loads are the easiest to find. You're charged these fees right up front—before your money is invested. Why should you pay? Usually because load funds are sold through brokers or financial planners who can also give you advice. Unless you're a complete novice, however, you can probably do your own homework.*

The quality of the fund doesn't seem to depend on whether or not it charges loads. And loads can run anywhere from 3 to nearly 9 percent of what you're investing.

Back-end loads: *These can be tricky. How do they work? Simple. You put your money in. No loads. Great, right? Not always. If you take your money out before a specified time, usually around five years, you get hit with fees, usually around 6 percent.*

Level loads: *These are just as they sound—consistently ongoing. So while you won't get charged a front-load (money up-front when you invest) or a back-load (money taken away when you withdraw), you will get charged a percent, typically 1 percent. This fee is in two* *parts: The 12b-1 fee that is used for marketing and advertising (no more than 0.75 percent); and a service fee (the remainder). Remember, this 1 percent is charged every year, not just at the beginning or the end, like the front- and back-loads. That means if you invest in a level-load fund for ten years, you end up paying 10 percent in fees. Ouch.*

Always look for the hidden and not-so-hidden fees of mutual funds. Even no-load funds may charge a 12b-1 fee that will run you approximately 0.25 to 0.50 of a percent annually.

And remember, you will earn less with a load fund, if two funds produce the same results. Loads eat into your money—and scant evidence exists to say that load funds perform better than no-load.

In addition to loads, mutual funds also charge *fees,* such as 12b–1 fees. These are sometimes called "hidden loads," because they can help eat up your profits. The name 12b–1 comes from the SEC regulation that authorized these fees in 1981. These fees cover marketing and advertising, and are deducted directly from the fund's assets. These usually range from 0.25 percent to 0.75 percent.

These 12b–1 fees are part of a fund's overall expenses. All funds have expenses; they're built into the fund. This is money used to pay the portfolio manager and transaction costs. Since they are built into the fund, the return you see in the newspaper is already adjusted for expenses, but not for loads or fees. You can always find out if a fund charges loads or fees by doing your homework. By law, all funds must list their fees at the beginning of the prospectus.

Where will you find these fund expenses? In the fund's expense ratio. This shows the total amount of charges deducted each year from the fund. This is a very important consideration when buying a fund. The less you pay in expenses, the more money will go toward your investment.

RISKY BUSINESS

A third caveat is our old friend—risk. Since most mutual funds consist of stocks and/or bonds, they are affected by the general market. That means some days you'll be sitting pretty and some days you won't. We suggest that you monitor your fund at least once a year to make sure the fund manager is the same and the fund's vision is still consistent with your objectives. Stay put until you reach your financial goal. Remember, the stock market will go up and down; the key is waiting out the down times. That's why mutual fund investing is for goals at least three years away. You don't want to risk losing your money in short-term fluctuations.

You also have to know your objectives, of course, and find a fund that's right for you. Since so many types of funds exist, know what you want, so you can try to meet your financial goals. Bascially, there are three types of objectives in mutual fund investing: *growth,* or increasing the value of your principal; *income,* or generating a cash flow; and *stability,* or preventing your principal from decreasing in value. Some mutual funds focus nearly exclusively on one of these objectives. Others may mix the three pretty evenly. To get the right mix for its objective, a mutual fund will invest in a combination of the three asset classes—stocks, bonds, and cash. While mutual funds are often categorized by their asset classes—for example, stock funds or bond funds—what's more important is the overall objective of the fund, or why a fund is invested in these asset classes.

Aggressive growth funds are for investors who are willing to take risks for growth. Index funds are funds that aim to invest at the index, or the S & P 500 level. Income funds are for investors who want to generate a cash stream.

WALL STREET WISDOM: ***Here are some helpful hints when considering mutual funds:***

If the fund has "growth" in its title, typically it invests mostly in stocks. If a mutual fund is growth oriented, it's looking for capital appreciation, or an increase in share price. Therefore, since we're looking at more growth, we're looking at more risk.

Another word to look for in a mutual fund is "income." If this is in the title, this simply means that the fund pays periodic dividends. Since this income helps to offset declines, these funds typically are usually less risky (and often offer less returns).

THE BENEFITS OF MUTUAL FUNDS

In a nutshell, mutual funds are gems for you, the investor with $5 a day. Why? First of all, you can get your money whenever you want it. That doesn't mean it might not be less than you want it to be, if the market takes a downswing. However, unlike CDs and Treasury bills, you can redeem your shares when you need the money. Many funds require only a phone call (on an 800 number) to sell your shares, and you'll get a check with the redeemed amount within a week.

Also, you can switch your money, sometimes for no or low fees, within a fund family, as your needs or goals change. A fund family is like any other type of family. It consists of different members who are related. So fund family Zebra might contain twenty different funds. They all are under the Zebra name, and chances are their management styles are similar. But like each member of a family, each fund has its own personality—in this instance, it would mean its own objective and portfolio manager.

Also, as we discussed in chapter 2, most funds will set up

automatic withdrawals from your banking account, or payroll check if your employer offers this. When you have a mutual fund automatically deduct money from your bank account or payroll, you are participating in *dollar-cost averaging,* which is one of the best ways to invest. You invest a set amount at a set time—let's say $50 on the fifteenth of every month. You never see the money, and therefore you don't miss it. When you dollar-cost average, you buy fewer shares when share prices are high and more when they're low. The result is usually a lower per-share average price.

WALL STREET WISDOM: *If you want to know more about dollar-cost averaging, T. Rowe Price offers a free brochure on the subject. Write 100 East Pratt Street, Baltimore, MD 21202; or call 800-638-5660.*

However, the greatest benefits of mutual funds include their professional management, diversity, and convenience.

Professional Management

Let's start with professional management. Although you always need to do your homework before you do anything on Wall Street (because a hot tip is only as good as its source), and this includes investing in mutual funds, a mutual fund company hires professional money managers to research and make decisions. These managers decide what investments to buy and when, and what investments to sell and when. And if they don't do a good job, they won't last long in their position. As a mutual fund investor, you are actually "managing the managers."

Just as different mutual funds have different minimum investment requirements, so they have different objectives and styles. And, although mutual funds are managed by professional money managers, these managers are not infallible. As always, you need to do your homework.

WALL STREET WISDOM: ***Although mutual funds lessen your investing risk, they still present the same types of risks as investing in individual bonds and stocks: market volatility, creditworthiness, interest rate instability. Also, a mutual fund can never guarantee results. They can publish how they have performed, but a high-flying fund can always dip if the market does. Also, mutual funds are not insured by the FDIC, like some savings accounts and CDs.***

However, the mutual fund investor does not have to worry about the mutual fund company going out of business. If this happens, the investors' money is safe. All money will be placed in accounts in a custodian bank under investors' names. The fund group or its creditors cannot touch your investment money.

Convenience

Mutual funds are easy to buy. All you need to do is pick up the phone and call an 800 number. The company sends you a simple application form, you fill it out with the appropriate information, including name, address, and Social Security number, send in the initial amount, and voila! you're a fund owner. This is where you can designate automatic withdrawals, too, so the money comes directly from your paycheck or bank account.

One of the greatest hindrances to buying individual stocks

(and probably where the saying "It takes money to make money" originates) are stockbroker commissions and transaction fees—the money it cost every time you bought or sold a share. But mutual funds are buying and selling many, many shares, and therefore the tranaction costs are spread among many, many people.

Also, mutual funds are efficient. Mutual funds provide you year-end summaries, so it's easy to include your earnings on your tax return. What counts as earnings in mutual funds are your dividends and capital gains. And since you usually have access to your fund via an 800 number, that means you can usually buy, trade, or sell your shares right over the phone.

Mutual funds also make it easy for you to reinvest your earnings. Mutual funds give you money in two ways: income dividends and capital gains distributions. Income dividends are simply the interest that the fund earns on bond or stock investments—minus the fees, of course. Capital gains distributions are similar—it's money that the fund is earning, but this time through the sale of certain investments within the fund.

Most funds will either pay you these earnings in a check or simply reinvest them into the fund for you, usually at no cost. Ravishing your earnings is a great way to make your money work for you and to pay yourself first. Chances are, you won't even miss these small amounts, and they can add up and really help your compound interest.

To enter a mutual fund, you usually need to pay a minimum investment. Mutual funds have minimum entry investments ranging from zero to one million dollars. The average minimum is $1,000 to $3,000. Many good, solid funds allow you to enter with a commitment to invest as little as $50 a month, even if their minimum investment requirement is higher. All you need to do is commit to investing a set amount every month until you reach the minimum amount.

We'll talk about this more later. But this option, usually called an *asset builder account,* is one of the best tools around for the small investor. Some funds have no minimums at all, but may charge a fee if your account falls under a certain amount.

Diversity

Since one of the best ways of avoiding risk in the stock market is by diversifying, mutual funds are a great bargain. Most experts recommend that you buy at least ten individual stocks in order to have adequate diversification to protect you from the risk of investing on Wall Street. A mutual fund can provide you with several hundred stocks for as little as several hundred dollars. Basically, mutual funds mean diversification.

That doesn't mean you shouldn't diversify across different mutual funds, or mutual fund families. You should. Funds are becoming more and more specific. Therefore, your best bet is to build a portfolio of different mutual funds—five is a good number—so that it contains different types of funds—for example, you may invest in an aggressive growth fund,

WALL STREET WISDOM: ***In addition to the resources listed at the end of this chapter, including the financial magazines, several associations offer assistance in gathering information on no-load funds:***

The 100% No-Load Mutual Fund Council publishes a director of no-load mutual funds. Call 212-768-2477.

The Mutual Fund Education Alliance also publishes a directory of no-load and low-load mutual funds. Call 816-471-1454.

an index fund, a sector fund, an income fund, and an international fund.

HOW TO CHOOSE A MUTUAL FUND

First and foremost you need to know why you're investing. If you're investing for a new car in three years, you might consider a not-so-risky fund, such as an equity fund or a mid-cap value fund. If you're looking at saving for retirement twenty years from now, you might consider putting your money in an aggressive growth fund. The risk is greater, but so is the growth potential.

So grab your time line. What are your goals? Do you want to go for broke? A lot of money with a lot of risk? Or do you want slow and steady growth? Do you want income? Have your goals in hand when you approach the counter to buy.

You also want to check out how well the manager has done. Remember, this is your money—you are, in a sense, the portfolio manager's boss. Be a good boss, be a diligent boss. Check out your employee's performance. If it's not up to snuff, shop around. How do you check out the portfolio manager's performance? Easy. Look at his or her track record. If the fund has made money under the manager during a reasonable market, that's good. If it's lost money while other similar funds have done well, well, that's not so good.

Basically, you want to track the one-, three-, and five-year total return of the fund. This shows the total profit generated by the fund. You can find this information either from the fund directly or in a variety of publications, such as the ones listed in the following Wall Street Wisdom box.

Remember, when a fund switches managers, you need to reevaluate the new manager and his or her vision. This doesn't mean that you have to sell the fund right away—

remember, every time you sell shares it's a taxable event—but put the fund on your "watch" list.

Find out what the new manager is up to. Give it a few months and then reevaluate. See what the manager is investing in, and how the fund is performing.

Ratings

Another nice thing about mutual funds is that someone is always keeping an eye on them. Since mutual funds are such big business, rating them has become a big business too. All you have to do is know the names of these rating services, go to the library, and ask the reference librarian to lead you

WALL STREET WISDOM: ***The following publications contain the track records of the top performing mutual funds. You'll also find the toll-free number of the fund. Keep in mind that you can only purchase no-load or low-load funds directly by phone. In order to purchase a load-fund, you usually must contact a stockbroker or other commissioned salesperson. (We recommend that you stick to low- or no-load funds, or your $5 a day will be somewhat less.) Always ask for a prospectus and the most recent annual report when you are considering investing in a fund. You can get this by calling the 800 number of the fund itself.***

1. Kiplinger's Personal Finance Magazine: *1729 H Street NW, Washington, D.C. 20006; 800-544-0155.*
2. Your Money *magazine: P.O. Box 3084, Harlan, IA 51537-3084; 800-777-0025.*
3. Money *magazine: PO Box 60001, Tampa, FL 33660-0001; 800-633-9970.*

to them. These publications will tell you what the experts think. They'll list how the funds have performed and what funds have fulfilled their objectives.

Here's a rundown of ratings guides. You'll find how the funds have done over the past one, three, and five years; investment objectives; how funds perform in relation to others; risk ratings; and fees, expenses, minimum investment requirements, and toll-free phone numbers so you can call and invest.

Morningstar Mutual Funds is the publication with the stars—the stars that you'll see in ads or brochures. They rate over 1,200 stock and bond funds in a biweekly publication. Morningstar lists a one-page report on each fund that they review. (Obviously they don't review all of them.) A five-star rating is best, with a four-star following closely behind. The ratings are based on best return/lowest risk ratio for category. A fund is rated along a bell curve with other funds of its kind. The top 10 percent receive a five-star rating; the next 22.5 percent receive four stars; the middle 35 percent receive three stars; the next 22.5 percent receive two stars; and the lowest 10 percent receive one star. Morningstar will also tell you what the fund's largest twenty-five investments are. Keep in mind that these stars are predicting not the future performance of a fund but rather how a fund has performed up until this point. Morningstar, Inc., 53 W. Jackson Blvd., Chicago, Illinois 60604; 800-735-0700.

The Value Line Mutual Fund Survey is another prominent rater of mutual funds. *Value Line* rates by number: A number one denotes a fund that gets the most return from the least amount of risk. Five is on the other end of the spectrum: the least return from the most amount of risk. Value Line shows how each fund did in up and down markets, and what the prominent holdings are. It also contains a written evaluation of the funds, and it rates more than 2,000 of them. Value Line Publishing, 711 Third Avenue, New York, New York 10017; 800-284-7606.

The Standard & Poor's/*Lipper* Mutual Fund Profiles rounds out the big three of mutual fund raters. This report covers over 1,000 funds and includes a half-page profile on each. In addition to yearly returns and largest holdings, this report also notes how the fund did in up and down markets. Standard & Poor's Corporation, 25 Broadway, New York, New York 10004.

READING THE PROSPECTUS

A prospectus lists all the holdings and activity of the funds, and mutual fund companies are required by law to make this information available to investors. It's a good tool for you, the individual investor, because it gives you one more way in which to judge a mutual fund. Sometimes a prospectus looks as inviting a read as your car manual, so here's what to look for.

Investment Objective: This is important. It tells you what the fund hopes to accomplish. Growth? Income? Politically correct investments? Educating its investors? Pay attention here. You want a fund whose objectives match your own.

Fees and Expenses: Very important. This tells you how much you will be paying to invest in this particular fund. This is where you'll see if the fund has a load, or if it's no-load. Make sure you check out the fund's management fee, which is what is paid to the portfolio manager. And check out the 12b–1 fees too. No 12b–1 is best of all, but a modest 0.25 may be OK. In this section you will also find wire-redemption processing fees and exchange fees.

Fund Management: A fund's past performance means little if it has recently changed managers. So check that out in this section. How long has the current manager been in place? The manager's style should be in line with your goals. In other words, if you are looking for a fund that specializes in small-cap value stocks—underperforming, smaller companies—then you want a manager who invests in these. Also, find out what the manager's philosophy is. Usually the fund manager will describe his or her investing strategies. See how specific and forthright these are. Obviously, the more specific, the better.

Performance: This is where you can see how this particular fund performed against others in its class. Usually this is done by comparing the fund to a relevant index, often the S & P 500. Has the fund over- or underperformed compared to the benchmark fund? Take a look at its performance year by year. Has it been consistent? Did one spectacular year buoy the overall average return? How has the fund performed over the last one, three, and five years? And, very important, check to see if the fund manager has changed. If he or she has, then the record means little.

How to Buy and Redeem Shares: This section helps you get started. You can find out how to set up an account with the fund, and whether you can buy and sell shares by the phone. Also, you'll find out how to set up automatic investments and how to make additional investments. You'll also find information on setting up retirement plans.

Rules for Switching within Fund Family: Again, this is important if you intend to monitor your portfolio—that is, change your investments from time to time according to your goals and the market. If you get a fund family that allows you to switch from the different individual funds without cost or penalties, that's a good thing. That way, if you need to switch some shares from an aggressive growth fund to a more conservative fund as your goals change, you'll be able to do this with less expense.

WALL STREET WISDOM: ***Some savvy investors let mutual funds do the work for them, in more ways than one. Not only do they invest in mutual funds but they also use the prospectuses and annual reports to see what individual stock investments the experts are bullish on.***

These individual investors choose the top-performing funds and check out the investment choices. And then they use these choices for their own portfolios. Keep in mind, however, that you still need to watch these individual stocks on your own. Not only does the stock market change rapidly, and the information in these prospectuses may be several months old, but you always want to have an idea of how an investment is doing before you take the plunge.

Risk Factors: This section is where you see what risk you're taking. This is where you'll find out what the fund can't invest in—and what it does. You will see if the fund invests in risky ventures, or borrows to invest in speculative stocks. Usually, the greater the return potential, the greater the risk potential. If you choose to invest in a fund, it makes sense to feel comfortable with its investment style and attitude toward risk.

Performance: Try to get a fund that exhibits consistency in management and objective. You will get updates on this, usually in quarterly and annual reports. The fund's president will write a letter stating why the fund has performed as it has, especially in relation to the performance of the general stock market. These reports will also contain how the fund did compared to other funds in its class, and you will get a list of the fund's investments, usually a list of the top ten holdings.

OPENING UP THE ACCOUNT

And then you get to start. First you need to get the prospectus and an application for all of the funds that you are thinking of buying. As we mentioned, you need the prospectus so that you know what the fund is about and if it matches your goals. Simply call the mutual fund companies and ask for these.

If you're opening an IRA in your mutual fund, you need to get an IRA application form from the mutual fund company. If you are transferring an IRA, you need to get an IRA transfer form. If you are going through a broker, discount broker, financial planned, or insurance agent, they'll provide you with all of this information. Otherwise, simply call the mutual fund company's 800 number and ask.

What do you need to fill out an application? You need your name, address, and Social Security number. You'll also need to provide the mutual fund company (or broker) with a check for the initial investment. Then, by checking the appropriate box, choose whether you want to have your income reinvested or sent to you by check. Again, we recom-

WALL STREET WISDOM: ***Time your investment right!***

When you first purchase mutual fund shares, it's important to do it at the right time. First, check the fund's distribution date—it's in the prospectus. This is the date, and it's usually in December, when the fund pays out its dividends and capital gains distributions to its shareholders.

After a fund pays these out, its net asset value—or share price—drops by the amount it pays out. If you buy into the fund right before the distribution, part of your investment will come right back to you as taxable income.

And that's not a good idea.

mend that you automatically reinvest your dividends. It's another way to pay yourself first. This is also where you can sign up for automatic withdrawals. Check the yes box, decide on the amount you want regularly deducted from your bank, and include a canceled or voided check. Again, we recommend this as a great way to dollar-cost average.

WHERE TO BUY MUTUAL FUNDS

You can buy mutual funds through brokers, discount brokers, banks, insurance companies, and the mutual fund companies themselves.

As you have probably guessed, the best way—read *least expensive*—way to buy mutual funds is through the mutual fund companies themselves. In fact, your best bet when buying mutual funds is probably to find no-load funds that you can buy directly without using a broker. At the end of this chapter we'll provide you with a list of solid no-load funds. You'll also find a list of funds that let you enter with low minimums.

Discount Brokers

Another way to purchase mutual funds—and individual stocks as well—is through a discount broker. Discount brokers are like those big discount department stores where you can get nearly everything you want on one shopping trip: You can buy all your funds from one place, with one phone call. You also get consolidated statements with all your account information and a consolidated tax 1099 form, although you will get separate forms for any mutual fund accounts you have in IRAs, SEPs, or Keoghs.

Keep this in mind, however: Even though you can buy or

sell the different funds from one spot, the discount broker will not provide you with specific information on the funds—the fund companies will do this. This means you won't get the free financial information from your discount broker.

Advantages of Discount Brokers

One mutual fund company may not own all the funds that you need to meet your goals. Of course, you can call the different companies separately, but the way to consolidate your mutual fund investments is to go through a discount broker. Discount brokers were first created as a way for investors to purchase individual stocks and bonds without the high commissions of full-service brokers. As a trade-off, they offered little or no investment advice.

With the advent of mutual funds, discount brokers evolved. Today, many discount brokers offer mutual funds without transaction costs. That means that you can buy and sell funds from different companies, or switch your money from one mutual fund to another, without paying a fee. Of course, you can also buy and sell individual stocks and bonds as well. And discount brokers often offer side accounts where you can park your money between investments. They also consolidate all your tax information in one handy statement. One drawback for the small investor is that discount brokers require a relatively substantial minimum to open a brokerage account, unless it's an account for a child (a custodial account) or an IRA account. Another plus to discount brokers is that most of them offer online services that allow you to buy and sell at even deeper discounts. You can also conduct research at their sites. Here are three well-established discount brokers and what they offer. All three offer 24-hour phone service.

Charles Schwab OneSource: 800-435-4000. Schwab re-

WALL STREET WISDOM: ***When do you sell a mutual fund? You're learning that it's usually best to buy and hold. Are there times when you should cut your losses?***

The following factors are red flags. While you don't want to jump in and out of mutual funds, neither do you want to stay with a sinking ship.

1. ***Your goals change.*** *This is the most obvious reason to sell a fund. For example, if you are twenty or more years from retirement, you will want to consider investing in growth or aggressive growth mutual funds. And if you are ten years or less from retirement, you may want to consider income funds or balanced funds.*

   The smartest move is to reevaluate your goals and objectives at least once a year to see if your investments match your plans.
2. ***The fund management changes.*** *A fund reflects its management: it's as simple as that. You may have a great performing fund that matches your return and risk needs. However, a management change could alter everything.*

   Your best bet? Take a wait-and-see attitude after a management change. Give the fund six months to a year. If you're not happy with its direction, it's time to change.
3. ***The fund performs poorly.*** *Don't confuse this with simply waiting out downturns in the market. If your fund consistently underperforms others in its class, you might want to look around.*

quires a minimum of $1,000 to open an account. They offer 1,500 mutual funds—nearly all no-load—and nearly 700 are no-transaction funds, which means it costs you nothing to switch in and out of them. A custodial account—an account you set up for your child—requires a minimum of only $500.

Fidelity Funds Network: 800-544-9697. Fidelity has its own family of funds—over 250 of them—for a total of 3,000 funds available through their Funds Network. Fidelity requires a $500 minimum. But no minimum exists for a custodial account, and you can set up an IRA for $500. Approximately 600 of the funds offered through Fidelity have no transaction fees.

Jack White & Company: 800-323-3263. Jack White's mutual fund network requires only a $500 minimum, and it offers nearly 6,000 funds, 1,200 of which have no transaction fees.

Online brokers: Another place to buy mutual funds is through an online broker. In 1995, only 12 online brokerages existed. Today the number stands at over 50. Commissions have dropped significantly; the average trade is under $20. They offer the same benefit as discount brokers—one stop shopping—at even lower rates. Some online brokers to consider include E*TRADE at www.etrade.com, DLJDirect at www.dljdirect.com, and Web Street Securities at www.webstreetsecurities.com.

WALL STREET WISDOM: *The Internal Revenue Service won't let you deduct commissions and brokerage fees. However online investors can reduce taxes by deducting cost of computer, internet service provider, and telephone costs. These qualify as miscellaneous itemized deductions, so you can only write off amounts exceeding two percent of your adjusted gross income.*

OVERALL OBJECTIVES OF DIFFERENT TYPES OF FUNDS

Different types of funds have different overall objectives. However, names aren't always what they seem, and the investment objective may not be readily apparent.

Risky Funds

Aggressive Growth Funds: High risk and high return. These funds focus in on capital appreciation rather than interest income or dividends. They are among the riskiest funds offering the potenital to make a lot of money, and the potential to lose, too.

Growth Funds: As with aggressive growth funds, these funds aim for capital growth rather than income. They are less risky, on the whole, than aggressive growth funds. These funds usually invest in the stock of well-established companies. Again, capital gains, not income, is the aim of these funds.

International Funds: As the name indicates, these funds invest in stocks and bonds from around the world. Some funds zone in on a specific area—Asia, for example—while others invest in a single country. Some exclude the United States; others, known as global or world funds, contain domestic and international funds. Diversity is always the key. If the fund invests in a wide range of countries, less risk is involved. The more focused the area, the more you're putting all your eggs in one basket. If a country's economy hits a snag, as Mexico's did several years ago, the fund will be jolted.

Small-company Stock Funds: Since we know that smaller companies typically have greater potential for growth than established companies, and greater potential for risk, these too are considered an aggressive and risky investment.

Sector Funds: Also known as specialty funds, these invest in specific industries or countries. You can get technology funds, a ''green'' funds (environmentally friendly), utility funds, healthcare funds. As you can imagine, there's less diversification going on here; therefore, more risk.

Growth and Income Funds: These funds aim to balance

long-term growth and current income. Generally, these funds invest in well-established companies that offer dividends to their shareholders. Less aggressive than aggressive growth funds, these still offer the opportunity for long-term growth.

WALL STREET WISDOM: *Part of the reason we keep suggesting that any type of stock market investing, including mutual fund investing, is for the long term, (usually defined at least three years), is that you can really get in trouble if you invest only a year or two, especially if it's in one of the more aggressive types of funds. For example, in 1973 and 1974, the average stock fund lost a total of 45 percent.*

Middle-of-the-Road Funds

Asset Allocation Fund: Asset allocation is a technical term meaning how you spread out your investments. You always want to allocate your assets—that is, you want to spread them out over different types of investments, such as stocks, bonds, cash instruments. It's a form of diversification. An asset allocation fund does this for you. It spreads its portfolio among a variety of investments, including domestic and foreign stocks and bonds, government securities, and even real estate. Some funds keep their asset allocation static—others change it as the market changes.

Equity Income Funds: These tend to favor income over capital appreciation. Therefore, they are less risky than growth and income funds. These funds invest in companies that have a solid history of paying dividends. Typical investments for these types of funds include utility, telephone, and blue-chip company stock.

Balanced Funds: A mix of stock and bond investments.

In fact, the allotment is pretty much divided down the middle. They are less risky than stocks, more risky than bonds. The goal is to preserve principal, generate current income, and provide long-term growth.

Bond Funds: Bond funds are also known as fixed-income funds. Generally, these are considered among the least risky funds. Bondholders have the first priority if a company sinks. But interest rates do go up and down, and bonds are affected by this.

Long-term Bond Funds: These are known by the length of the maturity of the fund's holdings. Most of the bonds in a long-term bond fund invest in bonds that mature in ten to thirty years. **Intermediate bond funds** mature in five to ten years. **Short-term** are less than five years.

Taxable Bond Funds: Another important distinction for bond funds is whether they are taxable or nontaxable. Since we know that municipal bonds are the ones that are nontaxable, these funds must invest in corporate bonds, or nonmu-

WALL STREET WISDOM: ***Here are some of the top tax factors concerning mutual funds:***

1. *When you switch from one fund to another fund within a mutual fund family—say, for instance, that you switch your money from ABC's aggressive growth fund into ABC's equity income fund after a few stock market jolts—the government will see this as a sale and purchase. Therefore, you must report your profit or loss.*
2. *When you earn dividends and interest (taxable, of course) on your fund, you must pay taxes on it.*
3. *Even if you automatically reinvest your dividends, you must report this as dividend income. (You must do the same with capital gains distributions.) Contact the Internal Revenue Service for their booklet No. 564, "Mutual Fund Distributions."*

nicipal government bonds. Again, with risk comes reward. What that means is lower-rated or non-rated bonds generally pay a higher interest. So, generally, high yield in a bond fund means high risk.

Very Safe Funds

Money Market Funds: These funds look toward money markets or cash equivalent investments—for example, CDs. Obviously, lower rates are expected, but risk is not a huge problem. Government-only money market funds look toward Treasury bills and short-term U.S. debt. They are backed by the U.S. government.

U.S. Government Income Funds: These invest in government securities, so they are backed by Uncle Sam. Typical investments include U.S. Treasury bonds, mortgage-backed securities, and government notes.

A LIST OF NO-LOAD FUNDS

The following are no-load, high-quality mutual funds. Whenever you're creating a portfolio, whether of individual stocks or mutual funds, remember to diversify across investment types and companies.

INTERNATIONAL FUNDS

1. T. Rowe Price International
   Toll-free number: 800-638-5660

2. Warburg Pincus International
   Toll-free number: 800-927-2874

Here's a picture guide to matching your mutual funds with your investment objective:

RISK-FREE

HIGH-RISK

Money market mutual funds	Intermediate-term bond funds	Long-term bond funds	Asset Allocation balanced funds	Growth & Income funds	Large-cap funds	Growth funds	Sector funds	Small-cap funds	Internat'l funds

3. Fidelity Worldwide
   Toll-free number: 800-544-8888

4. American Century-20th Century International
   Toll-free number: 800-345-2021

5. USAA International
   Toll-free number: 800-382-8722

LARGE-COMPANY FUNDS

1. American Century Income and Growth
   Toll-free number: 800-345-2021

2. Harbor Capital Appreciation
   Toll-free number: 800-422-1050

3. Vanguard Index Growth
   Toll-free number: 800-662-7447

4. Payden & Rygel Growth and Income Fund
   Toll-free number: 800-572-9336

5. Fidelity Growth and Income Oakmark
   Toll-free number: 800-625-6275

MID-CAP FUNDS

1. Brandywine
   Toll-free number: 800-656-3017

2. Strong Schaffer Value
   Toll-free number: 800-368-1030

3. T. Rowe Price Mid-Cap Growth
   Toll-free number: 800-638-5660

4. Dreyfus MidCap Index
   Toll-free number: 800-645-6561

SMALL-CAP FUNDS

1. Managers Special Equity
   Toll-free number: 800-835-3879

2. Eclipse Financial Equity
   Toll-free number: 800-872-2710

3. Nations Managed Small Cap Index Fund
   Toll-free number: 800-321-7854

4. Barron Asset
   Toll-free number: 800-992-2766

5. Longleaf Partners Small-Cap
   Toll-free number: 800-445-9469

SECTOR FUNDS

1. T. Rowe Price Science & Technology
   Toll-free number: 800-638-5660

2. Cohen & Steers Realty Shares
   Toll-free number: 800-437-9912

3. Invesco Strat Financial Services
   Toll-free number: 800-525-8085

4. Stein Roe Young Investor
   Toll-free number: 800-338-2550

SOURCES FOR MUTUAL FUNDS

Morningstar Mutual Funds: A compilation of data on more than 1,300 funds. Updated every other week. Subscription price: $400 per year or $5 per page. Morningstar, Inc., 225 West Wacker Drive, Suite 400, Chicago, IL 60606; 800-735-0700

Directory of Mutual Funds: Data on approximately 3,000 funds. No performance information, updated annually. Price: approximately $10. Investment Company Institute, 1401 H. Street, NW, Suite 1200, Washington, D.C. 20005; 202-326-5800.

Investor's Guide to Low-Cost Mutual Funds: Information on no- or low-load mutual funds, updated biannually. $500. Mutual Fund Education Alliance, 1900 Erie Street, Suite 120, Kansas City, MO 64116; 816-471-1454.

Individual Investor's Guide to Low-Load Mutual Funds: In-depth analysis of over 800 funds. Updated annually. Approximately $25. American Association of Individual Investors, 625 N. Michigan Ave., Suite 1900, Chicago, IL 60611; 312-280-0170.

The Value Line Mutual Fund Survey: Data on approximately 2,000 funds. Updated three times a year. About $300. The Value Line Mutual Fund Survey. Dept 6708, 220 E. 42nd Street, New York, NY, 10017; 800-284-7606.

Standard & Poor's/Lipper Mutual Fund Profiles: Data on approximately 750 funds, updated quarterly. Around $150

WALL STREET WISDOM: ***How to create a low-cost, diversified portfolio of mutual funds:***

1. ***Use dollar-cost averaging.*** *Sign up for a mutaul fund that waives the initial minimum investment if you agree to let them automatically deduct a set amount from your bank account each month (usually a minimum of $50). Not only is this a forced savings plan but you also get to take advantage of dollar-cost averaging, which smoothes the ups and downs of the stock market because you're buying more shares when prices are low, and fewer shares when prices are high. Normally, this lowers your cost per share.*
2. ***Keep your goals in mind.*** *Refer to your financial goals. Then decide what rate of return you'd like, and how much risk you're willing to take to try to get it. How long do you have to invest? Do you need income? Safety? Aggressive growth?*
3. ***Do your homework.*** *Read the prospectuses and annual reports of the funds you are interested in. Check out their objectives, their performance, their investments. Read financial publications that offer ratings of the different funds.*
4. ***Sign up.*** *You can't play if you're not in the game. Send for applications and fill them out. Include a voided check so you can take part in the automatic withdrawal programs. Let them reinvest your dividends.*
5. ***Build your foundation.*** *Make sure your foundation is sturdy. Start with a domestic stock fund. If you have a longer time frame, consider starting with an aggressive growth. If you have a shorter time frame, look to balanced funds or index funds.*
6. ***Start building.*** *Keep investing in your first fund until you reach its minimum. Then start to diversify. Choose a second fund with a different objective than your first. Then continue to add funds with different objectives or styles. Experts recommend a total of five or six mutual funds for diversification. Your best bet is to continue to invest in all of them regularly.*

per year. Standard & Poor's, 25 Broadway, Suite 1900, New York, NY 10004; 800-221-5277.

ASK A FINANCIAL PLANNER

In this chapter, Darryl Reed helps the clients enter the stock market through mutual funds.

Darryl Reed speaks: After Joe has begun to fund his savings account and retirement plan he then may want to get into mutual fund accounts. As Joe accumulates assets throughout the years, he can gradually move into each of these asset categories:

10 percent intermediate-term fixed-income assets
25 percent small-company funds
20 percent large-company funds
10 percent medium-company funds
30 percent international funds
5 percent REIT

Joe should implement his strategy by establishing a discount brokerage account at one of the larger firms, such as Schwab, Waterhouse, or Jack White. Not only can he choose from hundreds of no-load mutual funds, he can also set up a money market account for his emergency fund.

• Tess and David should invest as aggressively for Sonny's education funding as they do for their retirement funding. David and Tess need to make some assumption about the level of funding that they would like to attain over the next fifteen years. Based on their present financial situation, Sonny may find that he needs to take out some student loans, look for scholarships, or perhaps attend a two-year community college first. Time will tell. I would tell David and Tess that it's great to do what they can for Sonny's education, but I believe that their first priority is to make sure that they are taken care of during their retirement years. Sonny has many more paths and opportunities regarding college.

Over the coming years, they can continue to fine-tune the need for college planning. But for now they may want to start a growth mutual fund of $25 per month. More can be added to the account as their pay increases, holiday money comes in from relatives, or other bonuses come into play. Tess and David are also counting on Tess returning to work full-time in approximately three years. She is hoping that a position will open up at the local elementary school where Sonny will attend.

• For Carla, any longer-term goal, such as retirement or a house, should clearly go into mutual funds. If she has some say about the SIMPLE plan that might be set up at work, she can make sure it is done with a firm that allows her to pick from a wide variety of mutual funds, such as Schwab, Jack White, or Waterhouse. She should then refer back to her "master list" of investment mixes and determine which category to start funding.

• Marge and John should first take that $600 lump sum settlement and put it to work in a longer-term investment. Their retirement is likely to last twenty years or more, and they currently have no investments in the stock market. While John's pension increases from year to year, it probably won't keep pace with inflation. They need to start a portfolio of about a 40/60 stock/bonds split. They can start with a portion of their current cash flow and build in some of the money earned from their part-time income.

I'd recommend that they start with large-cap domestic and large-cap international stock funds for the equity portion. It will pay them a nice dividend and have some cushioning effect for volatility. The fixed-income side could probably best be covered with intermediate Treasuries or a combination of bond funds. If they feel like taking a little more risk, they might balance some of the bond funds with a high-yield fund. Risk is some-

WALL STREET REVISITED: **Checklist for chapter 5**

1. *Mutual funds are an excellent way to enter Wall Street on $5 per day. Your best bet is usually dollar-cost averaging, or investing set amounts at regular intervals. Many funds will waive their minimum initial investment amount if you agree to a dollar-cost averaging program.*
2. *Although mutual funds offer professional management (in additional to convenience and low costs), you still have to do your homework in choosing funds. Think of yourself as a manager of fund managers. You can judge funds by their performance records, their objectives, and their consistency.*
3. *If you have to choose between a similarly performing no-load fund and a load fund, your best bet is to go with a no-load. In general, no-loads are more effective for the small investor because more of your money is going toward your investment.*
4. *Even though mutual funds have inherent diversity, you still want to diversify across fund types and families. A diverse mutual fund portfolio will contain approximately five or six different funds.*

thing that John and Marge need to discuss, since they've never owned investments before. I would suggest that they read all they can on investing before they make any decisions. The library is always a good place to start.

SIX

Dividend Reinvestment Plans (DRIPS)

I'm a great believer in luck, and I find the harder I work the more I have of it.
—Stephen Leacock

DIVIDEND REINVESTMENT PLANS (DRIPS)—ONE MORE WAY TO ENTER THE MARKET ON $5 A DAY

Hopefully, you've already started to invest your $5 a day in a retirement account or one or more mutual funds. Maybe, though, you've always thought that to *really* be in Wall Street means to be invested in individual stocks, say in McDonald's, Home Depot, or Motorola. Of course, as you learned in chapter 5, you can own a share of many companies by investing in mutual funds. But what about those of you who want to fly direct? What about those of you who want to get the benefits of direct stock market investment—control over your portfolio, delay of capital gains tax until sell of shares, sense of ownership?

You could always approach a brokerage house and ask them to open an account for you so that you can invest in individual stocks. But what would happen if you went to a full-service broker to invest $5 a day in Motorola? The brokerage house may charge you so much in commissions that you'd be giving more money to them than to your investment.

And don't forget about diversification. Remember, most experts recommend that you own at least ten different stocks if you're going the individual stock route. And that can cost a lot of money. The smaller the number of shares that you buy from a broker, the higher percentage of your investment goes to commissions.

So is it true that only the rich can invest in the blue-chip stock companies, while the rest of us stay in mutual funds, 40(k) plans, and bank investments?

Nope. There's a way to invest $5 a day in the stocks of some of the best companies around. It's through plans called Dividend Reinvestment Plans, or DRIPs. They are perfect for the individual investor who feels comfortable making his or her own decisions yet doesn't have a lot of money.

WHAT IS A DRIP?

DRIPs, despite their name can be colorful, exciting—basically, they reflect the multitude of companies that offer them. In the most basic sense, a DRIP is a plan in which you are able to purchase the stock of a company through its dividends. Of course, you have to first be a shareholder so that you can earn dividends. Here's how it works: You buy one share (sometimes it's a bit more) of a stock in a company that pays dividends. And, instead of receiving your dividend payments by check, you simply let the company use your dividends to buy more shares of stock. In other words, you keep *reinvesting* your earnings. So you never have to buy more shares directly, unless you want to (and you will, because it's such a good deal!).

DRIPs are perfect for the $5 a day investor. And they're getting better all the time. One way they're improving is the ease with which you can now purchase your first share. For example, to take advantage of these plans, you have to be a shareholder already. Well, a portion of these companies—more than 300—now allow you to buy your first share from them directly, instead of your having to go through a stockbroker for these initial shares and using up part of your precious $5 a day. These stocks are often referred to as noload stocks.

Investing in DRIPs can now be as easy as investing in a mutual fund. All you need to do is fill out an application and mail in a check. Once you become a registered shareholder, with stock certificate in hand, you can mail your DRIP application to the plan administrator, along with an optional cash payment if you want.

Not only do these plans allow you to buy shares of their stock through dividend reinvestment, but the majority of these companies—approximately 73 percent of them—do not charge you commission to purchase these shares. That's the real beauty of the program. The remainder of the companies do charge fees (we'll talk about these later), but even these fees are far less than the commissions you would be charged to buy or sell shares through a broker, discount or full service.

And your options don't stop there: 95 percent of these companies allow you to invest more money, if you want to, every month if you want to. These additional investments are called optional cash payments (OCP). They are entirely optional, as the name suggests, and they can be as little as $25 a month.

WALL STREET WISDOM: ***What do you need to know before you can purchase a DRIP? (Tip: Whenever you need information on a particular company, call its investor relations department.)***

1. *The company's name.*
2. *The exchange where it's traded.*
3. *The minimum amount needed for optional cash payment. (Remember, you don't have to pay anything more than the initial payment if you don't want to.)*
4. *The name and phone number of the transfer agent: Most DRIPs are administered by a transfer agent, which is usually a commercial bank. The transfer agent performs all the administration for the plan: maintaining records, issuing and canceling stock certificates, and handling general issues for stock owners.*

WHO OFFERS DRIPS—AND WHY?

Here are some ground rules for DRIPs: First, the company must be publicly held. Second, the company must pay dividends. And last, the company must offer a DRIP. (You'll find a list of DRIPs later in this chapter.) Remember, not all stocks pay dividends, and not all dividend-paying companies offer DRIPs.

Well over 1,000 U.S. companies now offer DRIPs, and the numbers are increasing because the Securities and Exchange Commission (SEC) just made it easier for companies to establish Dividend Reinvestment Plans. Some market watchers are even predicting that DRIPs will soon rival mutual funds in popularity. Also, as we mentioned, over 300 of these companies offer you no-load stocks, which allow you to bypass the broker altogether and buy your first share right from them. We'll talk about them in a little bit.

You may wonder why you haven't heard more about

WALL STREET WISDOM: ***It's usually required that you use your own name, not a "street, or brokerage, name when you buy your first share in a company for its DRIP.***

If you register a stock in a street name, that simply means it is registered in the name of a brokerage firm. Therefore, the company from which you bought the stock has no idea that you are the owner. That's why most DRIPs require that you register in your own name. They want to know who their investors are. Some brokers may try to persuade you to register in a street name. Don't listen. If you register in a street name, the brokerage firm has control over your assets, and will most likely receive the commissions when the stock is sold.

If you already own shares in a company, and they are in a brokerage firm's street name, you may want to switch to your name when enrolling in a DRIP. Contact your broker.

DRIPs. In fact, they're sometimes referred to as "Wall Street's best-kept secret," because DRIPs are not a broker's best friend. They take money away from brokers—and therefore will not be high on a broker's Most Recommended list. However, the individual investor is becoming more savvy. That means the trend is toward do-it-yourself investing, which means lower costs and fewer commissions. Today, the list of participating DRIP companies reads like a Who's Who of blue-chip stocks: AT & T, H & R Block, Pepsi-Cola, General Electric, Johnson & Johnson, and McDonald's among others.

What's in it for the companies? Surely these companies have no trouble attracting the bigger investors, but that doesn't mean that they don't want your money, too. In fact, the smaller investors have their own appeal to companies: They usually invest in the company for the long haul.

THE BENEFITS OF DRIPS

With the advent of DRIPs, investors with $5 a day really have a full spectrum of investment options. Here are some of the benefits of these plans.

- You can invest small amounts without getting gouged on commissions. This is your chance to invest in individual stocks on $5 a day (and, for the most part, to bypass a broker).
- You are forced to save (really invest) your dividends. It's another way of paying yourself first. You can't touch those dividend payments. They just keep going to your investment. Perfect.
- Compound interest is in effect here: The more money you accumulate through dividend reinvesting, the more money that compounds for you.
- You can diversify for reasonable amounts of money. Remember, one of your best tools against stock market risk is diversification. Think of it as a life lesson: Don't put all your eggs in one basket. This way, if you are determined to go the individual stock route, you have a much better chance of owning the right number for diversification.
- DRIPs are basically dollar-cost averaging, one of the best tools around for the $5 a day investor. Just like dollar-cost averaging, with DRIPs you are consistently investing money to acquire larger holdings. If the market goes down, you're automatically buying low! You'll get more stock at the same price. Of course if the market goes higher, you'll get fewer shares for the same price. But as these things go, dollar-cost averaging typically works out in the investor's favor—a lower average cost per share.

And here are some lesser-known benefits:

• Some DRIPs offer discounts: Approximately 10 percent of the DRIPs offer investors a chance to buy the stocks at less than market price. How much less? Most offer the shares at a 3 to 5 percent discount. Some of the discounts are available for the initial purchase of the stock only, some for the optional cash payments. And some companies offer discounts on both. Some of the companies offering discounts include Berkshire Gas Company, FCNB Corp., and North Carolina Natural Gas Company.

Keep in mind that most of the companies that offer these discounts are either utility companies, real estate companies, or banks—all cyclical stocks. So be careful before investing. We'll keep repeating this: Don't go for the bargain alone. Make sure you are investing in a solid company.

• You can open a retirement plan DRIP: Some offer stock-based IRAs, and some allow direct deposit from your bank. DRIPs pair nicely with retirement plans; they're both for the long run. The opportunity to set up DRIP IRAs is becoming much more common, as more and more investors flock to DRIPs.

You will be charged a yearly fee for this service, usually $25 to $50 per year. However, as more DRIPs offer IRA options, more will start to offer "no-fee" IRAs. A few have already started—Atmos Energy, for one.

Here are some DRIPs that offer IRAs:

Atmos Energy Corp.
P.O. Box 650205
Dallas, TX 75265-0205
Shareholder Relations: 800-38-ATMOS
Plan administrator: 800-855-3040
Fax: 972-855-3040
URL: http://www.atmostenergy.com

Barnett Banks Inc.
50 N. Laura St.
P.O. Box 40789
Jacksonville, FL 32203-0789
Investor Relations: 800-854-5798
Administrator: 800-328-5822
Fax: 904-791-7184
E-mail: corpcomm@barnett.com

Centerior Energy Corp.
P.O. Box 94661
Cleveland, OH 44101-4661
Shareholder Relations: 800-433-7794

Exxon Corp.
5959 Las Clinas Blvd
Irving, TX 75039-2298
Investor Relations: 214-444-1000
Administrator: 800-252-1800
Fax: 617-575-2690

Mobil Corp.
c/o ChaseMellon Shareholder Services
P.O. Box 750
Pittsburgh, PA 15230
Adminstrator: 800-284-4100

Morton International Inc.
c/o First Chicago Trust Co.
P.O. Box 2598
Jersey City, NJ 07303-2598
Administrator: 800-990-1010

DRIP DRAWBACKS

Although DRIPs offer the small investor many advantages, you need to be aware of the drawbacks as well.

Timely buying and selling may be tough: You can't always sell—or buy—the stock quickly. Transactions are limited to the plan's transaction dates, which may be as infrequent as once every three months. A movement toward daily or weekly purchase programs is happening, however. Companies are trying to make investing in their stock through DRIPs as enticing and easy as investing in a mutual fund.

You are still taxed on the dividend earnings, even though you don't receive them in cash. Just because you are not receiving those dividend payments, doesn't mean that they are not taxable. They are. You'll need to keep every cumulative year-end statement you receive, to determine your basis in the stock when you sell.

Fees exist. Watch for them. Although you may be purchasing shares directly from a company and therefore avoiding paying loads, you may not be getting off scot-free. You may be charged a fee to purchase stocks through a DRIP. You may be charged a fee to sell shares. You may be charged an enrollment fee, or an annual administrative fee, plus a fee for every sale and purchase, including your dividend reinvestments. Some companies charge higher fees than others, so you have to shop around.

For example, at the time of printing, McDonald's Corp., Merck & Co., and Tribune Co., all charge both a small brokerage commission and a $5 fee every time you buy shares. If you're investing only $100, this would make a real dent in your investment.

Selling your shares may be more complicated than buying them. Sometimes, you can sell your shares directly through the DRIP. You simply put your request in writing—or you call in your request, as a growing number of companies are allowing you to do. You may have to wait up to ten days before the sale is made, however. You may be charged a fee for selling your shares.

Some companies won't allow you to sell your shares directly through the DRIP. What they will do is issue you a stock certificate (proof that you own the stock), and point you to a broker. Of course, you will pay more for this, because brokers usually charge higher commissions than the fees the DRIP would charge. When you sell, you have to figure out the cost basis of shares that you may have bought at hundreds of different prices. This is done to figure out your capital gains.

Also, you may not be able to sell just some of your shares. About half of the DRIPs offered do not permit partial sales. And if you bought your shares at a discount, you ignore that, because the amount of the discount is included as income the year that you bought the stock.

However, companies are trying to make DRIPs easier for you. They are computerizing their records, for one thing, and keeping records for much longer than they did before, in case you need help with your own record keeping.

Also, you can take advantage of computer money management programs such as Quicken, which help you track DRIP purchases. You just have to remember to enter each new purchase into the money management program. Alternatively, you can look to Evergreen Press, which publishes the Directory of Companies Offering Dividend Reinvestment Plans (see the resource guide at the end of this chapter). They offer a software program called Portfolio Tracker, specifically for DRIPs.

GRADING THE DRIPS

It may sound obvious, but just because a company offers a dividend reinvestment plan doesn't mean that it's an automatic buy. You still need to do your homework, and check out the stock and the company. After all, weak or inefficient companies offer DRIPs too. Remember what a dividend is: it's what a company can still afford to pay its investors after it has paid its operation costs and debts. But that doesn't mean that all companies that pay dividends are doing great.

You can rely solely on the advice of the experts, but we encourage you to do your own exploring. Read. And then read some more. Magazines such as *Your Money, Kiplingers, Money,* and *Barron's* routinely offer DRIP picks. Do some cross-referencing; see which companies keep coming out on top. At the end of this chapter, you'll find newsletters and books on DRIPs which rate them for you as well. And we're not above recommending that little-used commodity: intuition.

Visit the outlet, the store, the showroom of the company you're interested in. How do they treat customer? What is employee morale like? How do their products hold up? This is some of the fun of investing in individual stocks. And remember, investing is always a risk. Just because a company is doing well now doesn't mean they won't hit a skid in a year or two. DRIPs are for the long term, but don't be afraid to bail out if the company is flagging.

Don't forget Value Line, which presents a rundown of how a company is doing, including rankings of timeliness and safety. It's one of the most in-depth sources on individual stocks, and most libraries carry it.

WALL STREET WISDOM: ***What's in a prospectus (for DRIP investors?)***

Remember, a prospectus can be a handy tool. Here's what to check out from a DRIP perspective:

1. *Does the DRIP offer a discount on buying shares to its DRIP investors? If so, is the discount offered for dividend reinvestments or optional cash payments (OCP)—or both?*
2. *How often does the company make stock purchases for shareholders? Is it only at dividend payment time (approximately every three months)? Or more often than that? This is important because it gives you—the investor—an idea of how timely your purchases are. For example, let's say you send in an optional cash payment because stock prices have dipped: You may not be able to take advantage of the dip if the company only invests every three months and you're at the tail end of month one.*
3. *Does the company offer optional cash payments? If so, what is the least you can send in? What is the most? Companies differ—some allow minimums of $25, others of $500. Some allow you to invest up to $10,000 per month, while others cap you at $1,500.*
4. *How much does the plan charge its investors? What are its fees? Are you charged a fee for enrolling in the plan? For initial stock purchase? For dividend reinvesting? For optional cash payments? This is a crucial part of the prospectus. Some perfectly good DRIPs are rendered unpalatable to the small investor because of fees.*

GOING INTERNATIONAL WITH DRIPS: AMERICAN DEPOSITORY RECEIPTS (ADRS)

International investing is another way to diversify your portfolio. Often, the international markets move in different directions than the U.S. markets. If you are a DRIP investor and you want to invest overseas, you have several options.

One is to invest in U.S. companies that have overseas exposure. Another way is to buy American Depository Receipts (ADRs). These are issued by U.S. banks, and they represent foreign shares held in trust by a corresponding overseas institution. The ADRs trade on U.S. markets just as U.S. stocks do: You can buy and sell ADRs like you would ordinary U.S. stocks. You don't have to worry about currency translations. You are charged less commission than if you bought the shares directly on a foreign market. You can also check the stocks' trading prices in the financial sections and on electronic quotation services. There are some drawbacks, including currency fluctuations and the variance in accounting practices from country to country.

An increasing number of foreign countries with ADRs now have DRIPs available to U.S. investors. These countries may be hoping to gain name awareness and brand recognition in the United States. This means that you can buy international stocks on dollars a day, too.

The following is a list of American Depository Receipts that offer DRIPs. It is limited, but it shows you the range of countries involved—and the range of industries.

British Airways PLC; 800-428-4237 (Airline)
British Petroleum Co. PLC; 800-428-4237 (Energy company)
Marks & Spenser; 800-428-4237 (Retail)
National Australia Bank Ltd.; 212-648-3143 (Banking)
Nestle S.A.; 617-774-4237 (Consumer products)
SmithKline Beecham PLC; 800-882-3359 (Drugs)
Volvo AB; 212-754-3300 (Automobiles)

WALL STREET WISDOM: ***There are other ways besides a broker to purchase DRIPs not available through direct purchase from the company.***

1. ***National Association of Investors Corporation (NAIC):*** *The NAIC of Royal Oaks, Michigan (248-583-6242) is a not-for-profit organization that offers investment information to individuals and investment clubs. In addition to this information, members can also make initial purchases in nearly 200 companies with DRIPs for a setup fee of $5 per company. Membership is $39 per year.*
2. ***The Moneypaper:*** *This is a for-profit newsletter devoted to DRIPs. It offers its subscribers access to its Direct Stock Purchase Plan, which helps you purchase the first share. The newsletter also provides details, phone numbers, and rates of DRIPs, as well as an evaluation of the plans available. 1010 Mamaroneck Avenue, Mamaroneck, New York 10543; 800-388-9993.*

BUILDING A DRIP PORTFOLIO

Remember, you always need to diversify; even if you're investing only $50 a month in a DRIP, you want to make sure that you have enough different stocks in your portfolio to reduce your risk. How does the $5 a day investor do this? By starting small, and then building. Here's a sample start-up portfolio of diversified DRIPs. (Please note: names are followed by their listing the NYSE)

Most experts recommend at least ten different stocks if you're going the individual stock route. Also, with DRIPs, always make sure you are considering the costs of transactions. The following portfolio is available with an initial outlay of approximately $300, not including brokerage/transaction fees.

Definitely within each for the $5 a day investor.

1. **Abbott Laboratories/ABT**
   Minimum optional purchase: $10
   Company profile: Manufactures health care and nutritional products for hospitals and labs. Diversified products, strong growth projections.
   Investor Relations: 847-937-6100
   Administrator: 888-332-2268

2. **The Coca-Cola Company/KO**
   Minimum optional purchase: $10
   Company profile: Largest soft-drink company in the world. Largest distributor of fruit drinks.
   Investor Relations: 404-676-2777
   Administrator: 888-265-3747

3. **Wisconsin Energy/WEC**
   Minimum optional purchase: $25
   Company profile: Provides electric, gas, and steam power to parts of Michigan and Wisconsin.
   Investor Relations: 414-221-2345
   Administrator: 800-558-9663

4. **Motorola, Inc./MOT**
   Minimum optional purchase: $25
   Company profile: Leading provider of semiconductors and cellular phone systems.
   Investor Relations: 800-262-8509
   Administrator: 800-704-4098

5. **Home Depot/HD**
Minimum optional purchase: $10
Company profile: A chain of retail stores specializing in building and home improvement products.
Investor Relations: 800-928-0380
Administrator: 800-730-4001

HOW DO YOU BUY DRIPS?

If you are not able to buy the first shares directly from the company, your first step is to contact a broker or discount broker. When you express interest in a company, you'll receive information about the company—perhaps in the form of quarterly or annual reports, or the prospectus. You'll also receive an application for the DRIP. You must state that you are buying the shares to initiate the DRIP. Ask to be issued a stock certificate.

When you are a registered shareholder, with your stock certificate firmly in hand, mail your application to the plan administrator (which is usually just a commercial bank that handles the administrative stuff for the company). You might submit an extra optional cash payment (OCP) as well.

DRIPs are also known as automatic dividend reinvestment accounts because the reinvesting is done for you automatically.

Whenever you buy stocks, someone has to pay fees or commissions. The good news about DRIPs is that often these fees are partly absorbed by the companies. Always read the plan description to find out the fees. For example, if you are subject to a $10 transaction fee for every OCP, it really makes it less tempting to invest small amounts.

And remember, when you sell your shares of DRIPs, you'll

WALL STREET WISDOM: ***Advice for the DRIP investor:***

1. ***Look at the big picture.*** *Just because the DRIP offers a discount, low fees, and direct purchase does not mean it is necessarily a good buy. You still have to research the company by reading its prospectus, as well as other publications just as Value Line,* Your Money *magazine,* Kiplingers*—as though you were buying a regular individual stock. With the ever-increasing universe of DRIPs, you can afford to be choosey.*
2. ***Remember to diversify.*** *Even if you're spending only small amounts of money, diversification will help you hedge your bets. Don't forget to consider foreign companies.*
3. ***Maintain meticulous records.*** *Maintain separate and comprehensive records for every DRIP you own. You'll need them at tax time, and when it's time to sell.*
4. ***As always, consider using dollar-cost averaging.*** *It's a great way to pay yourself first.*

be assessed the customary brokerage fees and related sales charge.

We're taking it down to the basics so you know what to do from beginning to end. First, find out if you can buy the initial shares directly from the company or whether you need a broker. If the latter, then your first step is finding a broker.

You know the choices: either a full-service broker or a discount broker. A full-service broker will recommend a DRIP to buy, will execute your buy and sell orders, and will help you monitor your purchases. A discount broker only executes your buy and sell orders.

Shop around. Contact several discount brokers, as well as full-service brokers. Check online as well. Ask them what their minimum commission is. Let them know you want to buy only one share. (See Appendix A for lists of discount online and full-service brokers.)

Since the full-service broker gives you more service, you pay more. However, some full-service brokers offer special opportunities for one-share buyers. For example, Dean Witter Reynolds charges 10 percent of the stock price plus a small service charge. You may end up paying 50 percent less on this than if you went to a discount broker.

If you are buying your initial shares directly from the company, call their investor relations department via their 800 number and request an application form and prospectus. Once you have the application, fill it out and send it in with the initial payment. The minimum investment for these stocks is usually under $500, with some as low as $20. Usually, your initial investment will automatically enroll you in the company's dividend reinvestment plan. More and more companies that offer DRIPs—including Ameritech, Wisconsin Energy Corp., and Coca-Cola—are now also offering automatic optional cash payments, where you can have monthly payments deducted automatically from your bank account at regular intervals.

Right now, you can buy the initial shares directly from nearly 300 companies. Experts predict that these numbers will soar in the next few years, due to reduced regulations by the Securities and Exchange Commission.

INVESTING WITH THE BLUE CHIPS

DRIPs give you the opportunity to invest in those types of companies—the blue-chip firms—that you thought only the wealthy had a part of. Look at the following list that allows you to invest on a mere $25 a month:

Bethlehem Steel Corporation
British Airways PLC

Catepillar, Inc.
Coca-Cola Co.
Dayton Hudson Corp.
Goodyear Tire & Rubber Co.
Home Depot, Inc.
Intel Corp.
International Business Machines Corp. (IBM)
Mattel, Inc.
Quaker Oats Co.
Wendy's International, Inc.
Xerox Corp.

Since one of your best bets in investing is a regular, committed plan investing with good companies, DRIPs are a great deal. And optional cash payments in blue-chip DRIP programs allow you to do just that.

VIRTUAL ADVISING

When talking about DRIPs, where traditional brokers have little impact, the Internet seems especially pertinent. It's a do-it-yourself way to gather information on investing. Two sites in particular are oriented toward no-load DRIPs: Netstock Direct (www.noloadstocks.com) and the No-load Stocks Insider Home Page (www.noloadstocks.com) offer comprehensive information on companies that offer no-load DRIPs. In addition, Netstock offers direct linkage to the 100 companies that allow users e-mail access.

The following list includes fifty no-load stocks that are available nationwide. You can buy your first shares of these stocks with the companies, with initial prices ranging from $50 to $1,000. These shares go automatically into a dividend reinvestment plan. You can add to your account by sending in optional cash payments. When you're building a DRIP portfolio, aim for at least ten stocks. Make sure you diversify across industries. Also, just because the following stocks are no-loads does not mean that the companies do not charge fees. Consider all expenses when investing.

ABT Building Products: 800-774-4117
Airtouch Communications: 800-233-5601
Ameritech: 888-752-6248
Amoco: 800-774-4117
Arrow Financial: 518-745-1000
Bard (C.R.): 800-828-1639
Barnell Banks: 800-328-5822
Bob Evans Farms: 800-774-4117
British Airways: 800-711-6475
British Telecommunications: 800-711-6475
Cadbury Schweppes: 800-711-6475
Carpenter Technology: 800-822-9828
Central & South West: 800-774-4117
Conrail: 800-243-7812
Crown American Realty: 800-278-4353
Dean Witter, Discover: 800-228-0829
Dial: 800-453-2235
DTE Energy: 800-774-4117
Duke Realty: 800-774-4117
Enron: 800-562-7682
Exxon: 800-252-1800
Fiat: 800-711-6475
First USA: 800-524-4458
General Growth Properties: 800-774-4117
Grand Metropolitan: 800-711-6475
Hawaiian Electronic Industries: 800-543-5662
Houston Industries: 800-774-4117
Johnson Controls: 414-226-2363

McDonald's: 800-774-4117
Mobil: 800-648-9291
Nippon Telegraph: 800-711-6475
Oklahoma Gas & Electric: 800-395-2682
Philadelphia Suburban: 800-774-4117
Piedmont Natural Gas: 800-774-4117
Pinnacle West: 800-774-4117
Portland General: 503-464-8599
Proctor & Gamble: 800-742-6253
Rank Organization: 800-711-6475
Reader's Digest: 800-242-4653
Region's Financial: 800-446-2617
Reuters Holdings: 800-711-6475
Sony: 800-711-6475
Texaco: 800-283-9785
Tyson Foods: 800-822-7096
Uban Shopping Centers: 800-774-4117
US West Communications: 800-537-0222
US West Media Group: 800-537-0222
Walmart Stores: 800-436-6278
Western Resources: 800-774-4117
York International: 800-774-4117

SEVEN

Investment Clubs

CLUB—An assembly of good fellows, meeting under certain conditions.
—Samuel Johnson

WALL STREET NAVIGATOR: Finding your way around chapter 7

What investment clubs are all about
How to form your own
How to create a partnership agreement
How to create a winning portfolio
Where to go for help

WALL STREET ON $5 A DAY—AND A LITTLE HELP FROM YOUR FRIENDS

Now that you've been introduced to retirement plans, mutual funds, and DRIPs, here's a way to bring all of these investment vehicles together—and have fun while doing it. Investment clubs are another low-cost, low-risk way to diversify your portfolio. In this chapter, you'll find everything you need to know to effectively begin—and maintain—an investment club.

First, what are investment clubs? You've probably heard of the Beardstown Ladies, the group of gray-haired investing novices from a small Illinois farming town who now have books out detailing their investment strategy. Well, what they did is what the more than 120,000 other investment clubs are trying to do: pool their resources, give each other support, and learn all they can about investing while doing it. Members of investment clubs research stocks, make decisions, and commit to being in the market for the long haul. Also, these clubs allow you to diversify with more ease than if you invested on your own. You can choose mutual funds, individual stocks, DRIPs, and bonds.

Investment club membership has quadrupled over the past several years. And the investment club craze makes sense. After all, we're a nation of clubs: Boy and Girl Scouts, PTAs, 12-step programs. Investment clubs are another option for hardy pioneers who want to do it themselves. And investment clubs operate by the typical club rules: Dues, regular meetings, elected leadership, and a common goal.

Who belongs to investment clubs? Just about anybody. You will find clubs with only women, only men, extended families, church groups, alumni clubs. And like circles of friends, they can last a long time. The first investment club, the Mutual Investment Club of Detroit, began in 1940, and it's still active today. In 1995, the club's portfolio was worth over $3 million, from monthly contributions of $10 to $25 over its life. Members of the original club have come and gone, but the club and its original mission still exists: "The only purpose of the partnership is to invest the assets of the partnership solely in stocks, bonds, and other securities for the education and benefit of the partners."

WALL STREET WISDOM: ***Why are investment clubs so popular? Take a look at these statistics:***

A National Association of Investors Corporation (NAIC) survey of participating member clubs showed that the average return was 12.27 percent. The S & P 500 has historically returned 10.06 percent.

And while investment club members are not orangutans throwing darts to choose stocks (the quintessential image of the role that dumb luck plays on Wall Street), neither are they experts. See what you can do with a little patience, commitment, and discipline?

BASIC INVESTMENT CLUB TENETS

The founder of the Mutual Investment Club of Detroit, Frederick C. Russell, started the club because he was looking for capital to begin his own business. He had three basic investing tenets: invest regularly; reinvest all earnings; and diversify your portfolio. Think of the three basic tenets with which we began the book: commitment, patience, and discipline. Let's see how these qualities mesh with investment clubs.

Patience: Investment clubs are all about getting rich slow. The most successful investment clubs use dollar-cost averaging.

Committment: Investment clubs are not fly-by-night operations. They require long-term commitments, both to the other members and to the common objective. Also, when you join a club, you commit to active investing. This means that you go to the library and research stocks, that you read the business magazines and sections of your newspaper, and that you listen to shop talk (you too can become a complete bore at parties). But you'll probably never know what a derivative is, because no one really does.

Discipline: Investment clubs are not about impulse buying. It's hard to be impulsive when you're tied to at least ten other people. With all the structure and fail-proof mechanisms involved in democratic voting (although, true, we did elect Richard Nixon by a landslide), reactive buying, or impulsive buying, is far less likely. Also, most successful clubs reinvest all profits—that means dividends and capital gains. Again, you're practicing discipline, in the form of paying yourself first.

And don't forget about diversifying, a great by-product of investment clubs. How can you fail to diversify? You have other people to contend with—with their own favorites and investment styles. Also, the bigger investment pot that comes from pooling your resources makes it possible to invest in a variety of individual stocks, mutual funds, or even bonds.

CLUBBING IT

So, you've decided that you're interested in doing the investment club thing. First you have to find clubmates. How do you do that? Simple. Look around you. Look within your social groups, your family, your church, synagogue, or mosque. Choose folk you'd like to spend time with—this could be for years, remember—and also people you can trust to carry their part of the bargain.

Once you have interested members, you need to agree upon an objective and goals. You should put these in writing, so that prospective members know exactly what they're getting into when they join.

What might an objective be? As the Mutual Investment Club of Detroit stated, they were looking to educate and

WALL STREET WISDOM: ***The War of the Sexes: A truce?***

According to an NAIC study, investment clubs that include both men and women outperformed all-male and all-female clubs in four out of the five years from 1990 through 1994. (If we were to pit the all-women clubs against the all-men, the women come out ahead—they outperformed in four out of five years too.)

Another interesting development: Women are fast outpacing men in membership in investment clubs. In 1997, women outnumbered men in NAIC investment clubs 60 percent to 40. In 1987, the ratio was 80 percent male, 20 percent female.

benefit their members. That's pretty safe and vague. Others may be interested in more risky ventures, such as start-up companies. Other clubs may shoot for long-term growth. Maybe some investment clubs want to invest only in environmentally friendly companies. Try to find kindred spirits. You are pooling your money with others; therefore, you no longer have total control over it. It's a democratic thing. You want to find a good fit.

What are some of the things on which members should agree? Investment time frame, the amount of risk the club is willing to take, how many different stocks you want in the portfolio, and the amount that each member will be investing regularly. Once your club is established, you may want to invite new, interested investors to attend a meeting or two before they decide to join.

Don't be afraid to invite people who have different tastes and interests than you. That way, you'll be more inclined to have a diversified portfolio. And, as we mentioned above, coed clubs seem to perform better: Who knows why?

Your objective will be part of your bylaws. Your bylaws

will be a written statement of the who, what where, and why of your club. First you need to decide what investments your club will invest in. Mutual clubs choose to meet monthly. Then, where will you meet? What is the maximum contribution a member can make? How will members share in profits or losses?

Your bylaws are the heart and soul of your group. This is similar to setting personal goals, as you did in chapter 1. It's always good to have a road map for any investment journey. You will also need to set up an agreement—usually a partnership—so that your club can legally buy and sell stocks. You will also need to set up a checking account, find a broker if you choose to use one, and establish a name for your club.

Decide on how much monthly dues will be. Then you elect officers and hold monthly meetings. Each member is responsible for researching and analyzing stocks. You choose stocks to buy and sell. Sometimes you may hold educational meetings—invite a guest speaker, for example. Oh, yeah. You're also supposed to have fun and make money. This is the *Reader's Digest* version. Let's get technical now.

THE NITTY-GRITTY

Since the federal government requires that each club obtain a tax identification number and file the appropriate tax forms, you need to set up some legal parameters when you form a club. You have two choices, basically. You can form either a partnership or a corporation. The Treasury Department ruled that investment clubs typically do not meet all the requirements for being considered a corporation for tax purposes. Also, taxes and paperwork are less onerous when you form a partnership, so that's the configuration most investment clubs choose. And for start-up clubs, it's usually the best bet. (Corporations are usually formed to prevent liability. And since club members can do little with each other's money, liability isn't a huge risk. However, always make sure that transactions are recorded and entered for the whole club to see.)

In order to create a partnership, you merely have to write up a partnership agreement (we recommend that you use the Mutual Investment Club of Detroit's prototype at the end of this chapter as a guide) and fill out IRS Form 1065. Since partnerships do not have to pay federal income tax, each member of the club will be responsible for filing his or her own tax form at tax time (IRS Form K-1 will do the trick).

Your club may decide to hire an accountant or attorney to handle this paperwork. However, you probably don't need the help, if you follow these guidelines. You may consider hiring an accountant at tax time to help all members with their K-1 filing.

Your club also needs to open a checking account in the club's name. Also, you will need to get a tax identification number—Form SS-4—from your local U.S. Treasury office. In order to receive this, you have to provide the club officers' names, addresses, and Social Security numbers. As a partnership, your group doesn't need to pay taxes, but each individual investor does. You will need to appoint two or three members of your club, typically the officers of the club, to sign off on checks. You'll also need to get cash on hand, so you can pay departing members without disrupting the club's portfolio. Clubs usually get this through an initiation fee—typically around $100—and monthly dues. (This is in addition to the monthly investment amount.)

Since forming partnerships can be lucrative business to attorneys and accounts, you'll find professionals more than happy to assist you in your club's formation. For the most part, the extra cost and time aren't justified. All you need to do is use the form in this chapter as your guide. (Interested readers should contact the NAIC for a more in-depth explanation of the forms.) Make changes where appropriate, and make sure everybody reads and signs the form. So far, no legal activity has taken place with investment clubs.

Each club should have bylaws, and these should be updated annually. Your bylaws should have provisions for when the club ends, and how payments will be made to members. You should try to stay together for as long as the club is in existence, but be prepared in case circumstances bring unexpected changes in membership.

It's not advisable to allow any partner to become a majority owner; that's why limits are put on investment amounts. Also, some clubs charge fees for withdrawing—sort of like back-end loads that mutual funds sometimes charge. That way, the club will protect its own interests by preventing frequent withdrawing. Also, some clubs require a thirty- to ninety-day advance notice of the intent to withdraw—unless, of course, in an emergency.

Experience has shown that clubs do best when all members participate, as in most clubs that survive the first two years, which is usually the start-up phase. That's because you will have ironed out the kinks and realized that it requires more than desire and intelligence to make a successful club.

You shouldn't give up your personal investing just because you're in an investment club. Think of it as a supplement, a way to complement your own investments. Remember, always go for retirement investing first.

WHO'S WHO IN INVESTMENT CLUBS: CHOOSING OFFICERS

Following is a list of recommended officers. Ask members to volunteer for positions, and then hold a group vote to confirm or deny.

1. President. Also known as the presiding partner. Responsible for setting the time and place for the meetings, appointing committees, presiding over meetings. You want someone responsible and good at organizing and negotiating.

2. Vice president. Steps in when the president is unable to serve. Usually leads the investment education activities. Again, a leader type is a good choice.

3. Secretary (or recording partner). Keeps minutes of proceedings and notifies members of time and place of meetings. Also notifies absent members of activity by mailing minutes of meetings. Find a member who is detail oriented and conscientious.

4. Treasurer (or financial partner). Responsible for the club's financial records. Places the buy and sell orders with the broker or company if buying stock directly. Prepares a monthly liquidation statement. Keeps track of club receipts, disbursements, and calculation of each member's share of the interest in the club. The treasurer should also keep track of deposits and interest and purchases. NAIC's accountant kit

WALL STREET WISDOM: *How many investment clubs really exist? No one knows. The last time a real survey was done was in the mid-1960s. That total number was a quarter of NAIC's member clubs. Today, NAIC has over 30,000 clubs. So it's a safe bet to assume the grand total is over 120,000.*

will make things easier. Do we have to say it? Someone who has a head for figures is the one you want.

WHAT'S IN A NAME

You need to choose a name for your club. Since over 120,000 clubs now exist in the United States, it's sort of like belonging to the Screen Actor's Guild—you have to make sure there's not another Investors Anonymous, or whatever name you come up with, out there. So after you copy this partnership agreement from this book and make it your own, you have to call your state office. They will send you a form to register a name for a partnership.

They'll run your choice through a huge database and let you know if you weren't first.

HOW TO CHOOSE STOCKS

An investment club is only as strong as its members. Each member should play a role. The most successful clubs are the ones in which, at some point or another, each club member is responsible for preparing a report on a prospective stock. He or she brings the stock report in, and everyone goes over it before deciding to buy it. If you're a novice, though, how do you even know where to start?

First, experts say, look at the companies that you already know. How do you do that? Well, remember, this is the fun part—you're actually picking the stocks. So think about your favorite restaurant: Is it a public company? Is it booming? Do you think it has potential?

Or check out your favorite brand of shampoo, or cosmetics, or clothing line. Read all the time. What's hot? What do your kids, nephews, neighbors love? What are the trends? Follow your hunches—and then do your homework.

What will this homework entail? In the most general sense, it means look for a good balance sheet, consistent sales, and strong earnings growth. You want to buy a company that has a price-to-earnings ratio that is lower than its earnings-to-growth rate. Where can you find the P/E ratio? Look at the stock tables in the newspaper or online.

Of course, by now you know that annual and quarterly reports are your friends. Call the company's investor relations department and ask for an annual and quarterly report. Ask the investor relations department lots of questions, if you have them. If they are currently not making a profit, ask when they expect to, ask them how fast they think their sales will grow, and also who their competition is.

WALL STREET WISDOM: ***What's everybody else investing in?***

According to NAIC, the following are the top-ten companies in which their member clubs are invested:

1. *Motorola*
2. *Pepsico. Inc.*
3. *Merck & Co.*
4. *McDonald's Corp.*
5. *Intel Corp.*
6. *AFLAC Corp.*
7. *Coca-Cola*
8. *Lucent Technologies*
9. *R P M Inc.*
10. *AT & T*

RECORD KEEPING

One of the most important aspects of an investment club is record keeping. You have to track every transaction to the penny. And you have to keep track of each member's share. And keep in mind that some members may drop out, and others may join.

The NAIC offers an accounting manual, which has forms for recording financial information by hand. They also have an accounting software program. Some clubs hire outside accountants or bookkeepers to maintain the club's books. They will cost you extra, or course. Most accountants charge approximately $100 per hour. Who runs what? Well, the club's financial secretary or treasurer should handle the books. Most clubs do use accountants—but mostly for taxes only.

What are some of the complications in running a club? Some members may want to invest more than others, and you have to keep track of that. You also need to keep track of when members withdraw any of their shares, or a new member joins the group.

Everybody in the club should be familiar with the record-keeping process.

HOW TO RUN YOUR MONTHLY MEETING

Many groups make financial education their raison d'être. They'll attend education meetings and seminars sponsored by NAIC, or they'll take classes at local colleges. At the very least they'll read up on the market—this book, for instance.

In fact, this is one of the best things about investment clubs: You have to learn the basics.

You know, even though it might be fun, entertaining, diverting, and exciting, before anything else, your investment club is a business, and you've got to treat it like that. A good way to do this is through businesslike meetings. That doesn't mean you can't have fun; just have fun with the bottom line in mind.

First, you should meet at least once a month. And you should choose a consistent day: let's say the third Saturday of every month. Location can vary: You may rotate among members' houses or choose a coffee shop that lets you sit for awhile. Clubs that hold well-run meetings show the best investment results.

The same truisms for any successful meetings hold true for successful investment club meetings. Start on time. The meetings should have a set length of time; try not to exceed that time. Have an agenda. Old and new business should be part of the agenda. The treasurer should review the club's portfolio and give broker discussion highlights.

You should have a time to present stock analyses and recommendations. Each member can be responsible for researching a stock. Then you vote. You can hold an open discussion of stock choices. Club members should vote after the president or vice president motions to vote. Then you want to set up the next meeting: What will you discuss? What stock will each member research for next time?

At the end, when the important business has been discussed, cut loose and socialize. Don't forget to have fun—remember, this is a group effort.

TOOLS FROM NAIC FOR MANAGING YOUR CLUB

Your club will also have to decide if they want to use a broker. Most clubs do. The only way you can get around using a broker is if you rely entirely on mutual funds, no-load stocks in DRIPs, or take advantage of NAIC's Low Cost Investment Plan, which we'll talk about a little later. Otherwise, you need to decide do you want to go full-service or discount?

You remember the difference between discount and full-service brokers: Full-service brokers give you advice. They do the research, they'll help you choose stocks, and they'll charge you for the service. Discount brokers don't help you with decisions, but they're cheaper. If you do go for a full-service broker, consider using one who has worked with investment clubs before. You will do well with someone who listens to all members, who will educate members, and even attend meetings. Ultimately, the club has to decide for itself what investments to buy and sell. The broker is there to make suggestions, provide information on the stocks, and carry out transactions. Remember, the point of an investment club is to do your own research and make your own decisions. You might be skipping a bit of that if you go with a full-service broker.

When you choose a broker, make sure that you give authorization to the right club members, usually the officers, so that they can place buy and sell orders. But all members must sign an agreement when the brokerage account is opened.

Most investment club members belong to the National Association of Investors Corp. (NAIC), a nonprofit organization that provides members with a variety of support services, including a monthly magazine, *Better Investing.* NAIC has over 350,000 members, and the majority of the members belong to more than 30,000 investment clubs in this country and invest, on average, about $40 a month, or approximately $672 per club. The NAIC can be reached at 810-583-NAIC (810-583-6242).

In addition to providing an opportunity to invest in mutual funds, no-load stocks, and DRIPs purchased through NAIC's

Low Cost Investment Plan (more about this later), NAIC provides you with information-gathering tools. One is the Stock Check list. With this, you can record and review a company's earnings, sales record, and price history. Or you can use NAIC's Stock Selection Guide and Report, which is made up of five different sections. With it, you can record sales, earnings, and price performance over the past ten years. Then you can look at a company's management team. You can grade a company based on sales, earnings per share, pre-tax profit margin, and return on shareholders' equity.

In the third section, you can record the past year's high and low prices for the stock, earnings per share, high and low price/earnings ratios, dividend payout and yield figures. In section four, you can look to the future with this information: You can adjust these figures and estimate future prices. The final, fifth, section, is used to gauge ongoing results. Membership in NAIC is merely $39 per year for individuals; $25 per club, with an additional $14 per club member.

INVESTMENT CLUBS AND RETIREMENT PLANS

Yes, there is a way in which you can incorporate these two great $5 a day techniques: you can use your investment club

WALL STREET WISDOM: ***According to NAIC, more and more of its investment clubs are using on-line broker services—usually discount.***

NAIC encourages its members to buy stocks and hold on to them. The average lifespan of NAIC's member clubs stock holdings is seven and a half years per stock.

contribution as a way to contribute to your IRA—IF your club allows IRAs in its partnership agreement.

Of course, you always need a custodian when you set up an IRA. All this means is that a bank will have to agree to be custodian and act as a trustee and be a limited partner in the club. Since the trustee is a limited partner, the IRA trustee has no voice in the club's management.

If you can't find a bank who'll act as a trustee, contact the NAIC. The NAIC has a bank—First Trust in Denver—that has agreed to act as custodian for those who can't find a willing bank. The NAIC will instruct you how to change your club's partnership agreement to a limited partnership, in order to allow members to use their club investment as an IRA contribution.

NAIC'S LOW COST INVESTMENT PLAN

The NAIC's Low Cost Investment Plan is perfect for the small individual investor and the beginning investment club that doesn't have much to invest—at first.

Through this plan, you need to join the NAIC (of course), and they pay a $5 surcharge. Then, you simply invest in stocks *through* the NAIC. It's simply a way for you to purchase your first share of a company without having to pay a broker's fee. After that initial share, the NAIC pulls out, leaving the stock completely in your—or your investment club's—name. Then, the rest is pure DRIP action. You can add to your investment through dividend reinvestment and/or optional cash payments. You get started in a regular investment plan despite limited funds, and it eliminates broker's commissions, since the DRIP companies absorb administration and commission cost of purchasing the shares.

This is great, because oftentimes commissions can eat up to 10 percent of your club's monthly contributions.

WALL STREET WISDOM: ***Why investment clubs are hard work—and why that work pays off:***

1. ***You have to do your homework.*** *The NAIC recommends that clubs use its proprietary two-page stock selection guide (SSG) worksheet to analyze a companys' prospects before buying its stock. You have to plot historical growth in revenue and earnings per share, and analyze five to ten years' worth of data, such as profit margins, returns on equity and price-earnings ratios. After that, you project prices, dividends, and total returns. For the computer-literate, there is an electronic version. You key in the raw data, and let the software program do the rest.*

   Either way, investment clubs are conducive to investigating the market. This can result in a true understanding of the market and how to make solid investment decisions.
2. ***You may not make a profit at first.*** *You may have to pay start-up costs, which can include accounting services and software. It's also a time commitment. And it's investing for the long term.*
3. ***You have to prepare.*** *You have to get enough cash to set up an account, you have to get a broker, and you have to address issues you need to face when setting up a business.*

   This can result in learning how to run your own investment portfolio. It will decrease your chances of being at the mercy of "experts."
4. ***You have to work with others, and you have to be open to others.*** *The best investment clubs have membership that is diverse in terms of age, background, experience, and gender.*

   This can result in learning how to work effectively with others and expanding your view of investing—and the world.

MORE INS AND OUTS OF CLUBS

Here are some last words of advice for investment clubs.

• Keep membership to a reasonable number. Makes sense, right? You can't have too small, or too unruly, a crowd. So what's reasonable? Most experts advise a membership of ten to twenty. If you go larger, it may be hard to reach decisions. If you go smaller, you have less cash to work with. Also, many hands make light work. Too few members leave you to do more work.

• Make sure that everyone can afford the monthly investment amount. After an initial inductee fee, keep your investment amount in the range of $25 to $50 a month. Remember, if you have $100 more a month, you can always invest outside of a club.

• An investment club is not a mutual fund. Everyone has to work, and each prospective member needs to understand this. The club should have bylaws that deal with members unwilling to shoulder their share of the work.

• Keep other investments, apart from your investment club ventures. This isn't exactly essential, but it makes sense. It's always nice to diversify, and this gives you one more way to do it.

PARTNERSHIP OF THE MUTUAL INVESTMENT CLUB OF DETROIT

THIS AGREEMENT OF PARTNERSHIP, effective as of (DATE), by and between the undersigned, to wit:

(Name of all partners)

NOW, THEREFORE, IT IS AGREED:

1. Formation. The undersigned hereby form a General Partnership in accordance with and subject to the laws of the State of Michigan.

2. Name. The name of the partnership shall be Mutual Investment Club of Detroit.

3. Term. The partnership will begin on (DATE) and shall continue until December 31 of the same year and thereafter from year to year unless earlier terminated as hereinafter provided.

4. Purpose. The only purpose of the partnership is to invest the assets of the partnership solely in stocks, bonds, and other securities for the education and benefit of the partners.

5. Meetings. Periodic meetings shall be held as determined by the partnership.

6. Capital Contributions. The partners may make capital contributions to the partnership on the date of each periodic meeting in such amounts as the partnership shall determine, provided, however, that no partner's capital account shall exceed twenty percent (20%) of the capital accounts of all the partners.

7. Value of the Partnership. The current value of the assets of the partnership, less the current value of the liabilities of the partnership (hereinafter referred to as ''value of the partnership'') shall be determined as of regularly scheduled date and time (''valuation date'') preceding the date of each periodic meeting determined by the Club.

8. Capital Accounts. A capital account shall be maintained in the name of each partner. Any increase or decrease in the value of the partnership on any valuation date shall be credited or debited, respectively, to each partner's capital account in proportion to the

sum of all partner's capital accounts on that date. Any other method of valuating each partner's capital account may be substituted for this method, provided the substituted method results in exactly the same valuation as previously provided herein. Each partner's capital contribution to, or capital withdrawal from, the partnership, shall be credited, or debited, respectively, to that partner's capital account.

9. Management. Each partner shall participate in the management and conduct of the affairs of the partnership in proportion to the value of his capital account. Except as otherwise determined, all decisions shall be made by the partners whose capital accounts total a majority of the value of the capital accounts of all partners.

10. Sharing of Profits and Losses. Net profits and losses of the partnership shall inure to, and be borne by, the partners in proportion to the value of each of their capital accounts.

11. Books of Accounts. Books of accounts of the transactions of the partnership shall be kept and at all times be available and open to inspection and examination by any partner.

12. Annual Accounting. Each calendar year, a full and complete account of the condition of the partnership shall be made to the partners.

(Drawing up an agreement like this one will provide your Club with a written statement of your procedures and processes.)

13. Bank Account. The partnership may select a bank for the purpose of opening a bank account. Funds in the bank account shall be withdrawn by checks signed by any partner designated by the partnership.

14. Broker Account. None of the partners of this partnership shall be a broker. However, the partnership may select a broker and enter into such agreements with the broker as required for the purchase or sale of securities. Securities owned by the partnership

shall be held in the partnership name unless another name shall be designated by the partnership.

At the time of a transfer of securities, the corporation or transfer agent is entitled to assume (1) that the partnership is still in existence, and (2) that this Agreement is in full force and effect and has not been amended unless the corporation or transfer agent has received written notice to the contrary.

15. No Compensation. No partner shall be compensated for services rendered to the partnership, except reimbursement for expenses.

16. Additional Partners. Additional partners may be admitted at any time, upon the unanimous consent of all the partners, so long as the number of partners does not exceed twenty-five (25).

16A. Transfers to a Trust. A partner may, after giving written notice to the other partners, transfer his interest in the partnership to a revocable living trust of which he is the grantor and sole trustee.

16B. Removal of a Partner. Any partner may be removed by agreement of the partners whose capital accounts total a majority of the value of all partners' capital accounts. Written notice of a meeting where removal of a partner is to be considered shall include a specific reference to this matter. The removal shall become effective upon payment of the value of the removed partner's capital account, which shall be in accordance with the provisions on full withdrawal of a partner noted in paragraphs 18 and 20. The vote action shall be treated as receipt of request for withdrawal.

17. Termination of Partnership. The partnership may be terminated by agreement of the partners whose capital accounts total a majority in value of the capital accounts of all the partners. Written notice of the meeting where termination of the partnership is to be considered shall include a specific reference to this matter. The partnership shall terminate upon a majority vote of all partners' capital

accounts. Written notice of the decision to terminate the partnership shall be given to all the partners. Payment shall then be made of all the liabilities of the partnership and a final distribution of the remaining assets either in cash or in kind, shall promptly be made to the partners of their personal representatives in proportion to each partner's capital account.

18. Voluntary Withdrawal (Partial or Full) of a Partner. Any partner may withdraw a part or all of the value of his capital account in the partnership and the partnership shall continue as a taxable entity. The partner withdrawing a portion or all of the value of his capital account shall give notice of such intention in writing to the Secretary. Written notice shall be deemed to be received as of the first meeting of the partnership at which it is presented. If written notice is received between meetings it will be treated as received at the first following meeting.

In making payment, the value of the partnership as set forth in the valuation statement prepared for the first meeting following the meeting at which written notice is received from a partner's capital account. The partnership shall pay the partner who is withdrawing a portion or all of the value of his capital account in the partnership in accordance with paragraph 20 of the Agreement.

19. Death or Incapacity of a Partner. In the event of the death or incapacity of a partner (or the death or incapacity of the grantor and sole trustee of a revocable living trust, if such trust is a partner pursuant to Paragraph 16A hereof), receipt of notice of such an event shall be treated as notice of full withdrawal.

20. Terms of Payment. In the case of a partial withdrawal, payment may be made in cash or securities of the partnership or a mix of each at the option of the partner making the partial withdrawal. In the case of a full withdrawal, payments may be made in cash or securities or a mix of each at the option of the remaining partners.

In either case, where securities are to be distributed, the remaining partners select the securities.

Where cash is transferred, the partnership shall transfer to the partner (or other appropriate entity) withdrawing a portion of all of his interest in the partnership, an amount equal to the lesser of (i) ninety-seven percent (97%) of the value of the capital account in the partnership being withdrawn or (ii) the value of the capital account being withdrawn, less the actual cost to the partnership of selling securities to obtain cash to meet the withdrawal. The amount being withdrawn shall be paid within 10 days after the evaluation date used in determining the withdrawal amount.

If a partner withdrawing a portion or all of the value of his capital account in the partnership desires an immediate payment in cash, the partnership at its earliest convenience may pay eighty percent (80%) of the estimated value of his capital account and settle the balance in accordance with valuation and payment procedures set forth in paragraphs 18 and 20.

When securities are transferred, the partnership shall select securities to transfer equal to the value of the capital account or a portion of the capital account in the partnership. The Club's broker shall be advised that ownership of the securities has been transferred to the partner as of the valuation date used for the withdrawal.

21. Forbidden Act: No partner shall:
(a) Have the right or authority to bind or obligate the partnership to any extent whatsoever with regard to any matter outside the scope of the partnership purpose.

(b) Except as provided in paragraph 16A, without the unanimous consent of all the other partners, assign, transfer, pledge, mortgage or sell all or part of his or her interest in the partnership to any other partner or other person whomsoever, or enter into agreement as the result of which any person or persons not a partner shall become interested with him in the partnership.

(c) Purchase an investment for the partnership where less than the full purchase price is paid for the same.

(d) Use the partnership name, credit, or property for other than partnership purposes.

(e) Do any act detrimental to the interests of the partnership or which would make it impossible to carry on the purpose of the partnership.

This Agreement of Partnership shall be binding upon the respective heirs, executors, trustees, administrators and personal representatives of the partners.

The partners have caused the Agreement of Partnership to be executed on the dates indicated below, effective as of the date indicated above.

OPERATING PROCEDURE
MUTUAL INVESTMENT CLUB

Duties of Partners

Annually, at the first meeting in February, partners shall elect the following positions and assign duties as described below by a majority vote:

1. President. The President's duty is to preside over meetings, set meeting dates and locations, appoint committees and see that resolutions passed by the partnership are carried out.

2. Vice President. The Vice President takes the place of the President when the President is absent or incapacitated. The Vice Presi-

dent shall assign companies to report on at Club meetings to each partner and shall be responsible for insuring that the Club's study program is properly carried out.

3. Secretary. The Secretary's duty is to keep a record of the actions authorized by the partners and notify partners of meetings and other activities.

4. Treasurer. The Treasurer's duty is to keep a record of the Club's receipts and disbursements and partners' interests in the Club. The Treasurer will give partners receipts for payments, place the buy and sell orders authorized by the partners with the Club's broker, and prepare the Club's monthly Valuation Statement. He will see that the needed tax information is compiled and file the necessary reports.

Guests

Partners may invite guests to any meeting of the Club as long as advance clearance is obtained from the host of the meeting. When consideration is given to adding partners to the Club under paragraph 16 or the Club's partnership agreement, anyone considering shall have been a guest for at least two prior meetings.

Meetings

The Club shall hold a meeting on the second Tuesday of each month at a place designated by the Club. Written notice of each meeting shall be given to each partner by the Secretary at least one week before the meeting. Special meetings may be called by the President upon similar notice to the other partners.

PROCEDURE

The monthly valuation statement shall be effective as of a regularly scheduled date and time preceding each monthly meeting.

In maintaining the records of each partner's capital account in the Club, the unit value method as outlined in Chapter 21 of this manual will be used.

Additional deposits in the Club may be made by members in multiples of $10.

The Vice President shall contact investment counsel immediately preceding the monthly meeting and secure investment counsel's suggestions on new companies to consider, and any comments on stocks owned by the Club. He shall report this information at the meeting. The Vice President shall appoint at least two partners at each meeting to prepare a report on the NAIC Stock Selection Guide on a security for presentation to the partnership at the following meeting. The Vice President shall remind each person assigned to prepare an NAIC Stock Selection Guide of his assignment one week before the meeting.

Buy and/or sell action may be taken after a period of discussion by the members, and when voted by a simple majority of the members' interests.

End of motion.

WALL STREET SMARTS: THE STEP-TO-STEP GUIDE TO INVESTMENT CLUBS:

1. Find fellow club members. Try to keep your club between ten and twenty members. Find people you trust and with whom you wouldn't mind having a long-term association.

2. Agree on an objective.
3. Form a partnership. Don't forget to include an IRA provision if club members are interested.
4. Elect officers.
5. Get a federal Tax ID number.
6. Open a checking account.
7. Create bylaws that include meeting schedule, dues, monthly amount invested.
8. Find a broker (if you need one).
9. Join the NAIC (if you choose to).
10. Give each member stock researching responsibilities.
11. Build a portfolio that is stable and growth-oriented.
12. Keep an eye on the portfolio.
13. Educate yourselves.
14. Update bylaws annually.

EIGHT

Twenty Questions for the Future

Used rightly, money allows us to live, eat, drink, protect ourselves, help our families and friends, maintain our health, accomplish certain aims. This it does by reconciling external conflicts, by allowing relationships and exchanges to exist between elements that are not yet in relationship. It can be an instrument of love, hate, challenge, tenderness—all the normal feelings of a normal human being.

—Jacob Needleman

Congratulations. You've made it to Wall Street. You've learned enough to embark on your own investing plan. All it needs is your $5 a day—and your commitment, patience, and discipline. Fortunately, Wall Street is sprinkled with enough success stories to give you faith. Many of the most effective investors have done it themselves, on dollars a day.

However, one thing about being successful at any type of endeavor is that success brings on more challenges. Investing is no different. It is truly a lifelong process. Once you have your portfolio in place, you need to keep an eye on it, make sure it changes as your life and goals do, and nurture it as it grows. So we've compiled a list of commonly asked questions to help you in this process. We hope these help you as you travel your path toward financial stability.

Happy trails.

NOW WHAT? INFORMATION TO HELP YOU MANAGE YOUR PORTFOLIO

Q: What do I do when the stock market falls, and the prices of my investments go down?

A: Although any investment decision is a personal one, most experts agree that riding out the stock market's volatility will suit you better over the long haul than jumping in and out. If a market dive keeps you up at night, it's no good hanging on to your investments and sacrificing your peace of mind. *However,* the stock market will go up and down by its very nature. Remember, the historic return of the stock market is 10 percent. You won't always see this return from one year to the next, but you're likely to see it over the long run.

Q: What action should I take in my investment portfolio when major life changes occur?

A: At the absolute minimum, you should monitor your portfolio once a year. If you can, review it every six months. First review your life. Has anything changed? Have you gotten married? Did you have a child? Were you divorced? Has a relative become dependent on you? Look at anything that will impact immediately or potentially the amount of money you'll need to survive. Then look at your portfolio again to see if it's allocated appropriately for your new financial responsibilities. Let's run through a few of the major life changes and what you need to look at.

Marriage: First, have an open discussion with your spouse concerning financial goals and assets. You need to agree on your combined goals and financial strategies. You also need to change your retirement and insurance plan beneficiaries. (This is especially important in the event of a second marriage.) Look at the titling of each type of investment account and determine if joint ownership makes sense. Look at your combined investments and see if there are overlaps. Also look at what you both earn and how you both spend. Who has what coming in, and who is going to pay what bills? Discuss whether you want a joint checking account. The four big financial issues that couples face are determining goals; paying the bills; keeping a budget; and setting up a savings and investing plan. By facing these issues head on, you're starting your marriage off on the right foot.

Birth of a child: First of all, did you get a Social Security number? Have you wills in place in case anything happens to you or your spouse? Have you named guardians? Revisit your cash flow. What do you need to alter if you want to begin funding your child's college education?

Raise/promotion: One good rule of thumb with a raise or promotion is to spend half and save or invest the other half. Look at your current cash flow. Do you have a financial goal, such as paying down debt, that you want to accelerate? Take a look at your goals. Has anything changed in your life? Does your current asset allocation make sense? Where can you invest more? Look at the big picture of your portfolio: Are you lacking presence in any particular market sector, such as international investments? Fund that part of your portfolio.

Divorce: You're going from a family unit that had its own goals and assets to an individual situation or another family unit. Are your objectives the same? Is the cash flow the same? After the assets have been divided, you need to completely review your goals and investment choices.

At every new point in your life, you want to ask the following questions: What are my goals? What are my target rate of returns? What is my risk tolerance? Keep it simple. The best way to manage a portfolio is with grace and simplicity.

Q: For how long do I have to keep my tax documents?

A: Six years seems to be the magic date. The IRS has three years from the date you file your return to audit your return if it suspects a "good faith" error. This three-year deadline works for you too. If you find an error, and want to claim a refund, you can do so in that time period. The IRS has six years in which to audit your return if it feels you underreported your income by 25 percent or more. There's no time limit if the IRS thinks you failed to file a return, or if they think you filed a fraudulent return.

Therefore, it's a good idea to keep your returns, including your W-2 forms and 1099s, canceled checks, receipts for alimony, contributions, child care, medical expenses, retirement plan contributions, mortgage interest—anything that you claim on your returns—for six years. The IRS offers a free brochure, Publication 552, called "Recordkeeping for Individuals." Call 800-829-3676.

WALL STREET WISDOM: ***The five risks to avoid:***

1. **Building an investment portfolio without laying the groundwork first.** *Without adequate insurance or an accessible savings plan, you risk interrupting your long-term investing. Or, worse, you risk losing all your assets to an emergency situation.*
2. **Playing it too safe.** *"Safe" investments—such as savings accounts or bonds—are a greater risk than we realize. They're a necessary part of any portfolio, but they don't hedge against inflation.*

   And inflation is a fact of life. It puts you at risk for loss of purchasing power. What may look like a lot of money to you today may not even be enough to buy a few lottery tickets twenty years down the road. Therefore, while fixed-income investments are a necessary part of any portfolio, keep a good portion of your investments in the stock market for your long-term goals.
3. **Timing the market.** *Instead of trying to buy low and sell high, or timing the market, reduce your long-term investing risk by using dollar-cost averaging. Simply invest a predetermined, fixed amount of money every month. Not only are you forced to invest regularly, but since you buy more shares in periods of lower prices and fewer shares in periods of high prices, you spread your risk over time. It also keeps you in the market for the long term, which helps you take advantage of your greatest ally: Time.*
4. **Procrastinating.** *Since the real power in investing is time, just do it. You lose valuable compound interest every day that you wait.*
5. **Buying only one or two stocks or buying only one asset class.** *If you own stocks or mutual funds in only one category, you're setting yourself up for a fall. Owning five aggressive growth mutual funds, for example, doesn't provide diversification. Funds that invest for the same objective generally will be affected by the same set of factors. We can't say this enough. Diversify, diversify, diversify.*

Q: How are taxes handled with Dividend Reinvestment Plans (DRIPs)?

A: The dividends that are generated by your DRIP investment are reported as taxable income, even when you reinvest the money to buy more shares of the stock. You only have to report capital gains if you sell the stock. The plan administrator will send you form 1099-DIV in January of each year listing the dividends and other distributions received. You will also have to report any fees paid by the company on your behalf, such as brokerage commissions. You do not have to pay taxes on additional shares if your stock splits.

Q: How do I choose an individual stock?

A: One of the tricky things about individual stocks, whether you buy them through a broker or directly from the company in a Dividend Reinvestment Plan, is that you need to diversify. A rule of thumb is to not place more than 20 percent of your total assets in the stock of one company.

Here are some guidelines to judging a stock:

1. See if the overall trend of the *earnings per share,* or the company's net income divided by the average number of common stocks outstanding, has increased over the past five years. This is listed in the company's annual report or reference materials such as Value Line.
2. See if the dividends have increased over the past five years. Increased dividends are a good sign.
3. Consider the company's P/E ratio, or the price to earnings ratio. You determine this ratio by dividing the previous year's earnings per share into the current price of the stock. The P/E ratio reflects inves-

tor confidence in a stock. A P/E ratio under 10 is considered conservative. Above 10, you begin to pay more for the company's future. Although a lower P/E ratio may connote uncertainty about a company's future, you want to get in on as low a P/E as possible—before there is a lot of investor interest.

Q: What are some college planning strategies?

A: **Zero coupon bonds:** Zero coupon bonds are municipal, corporate, and Treasury bonds without their interest coupons. Thus, unlike regular bonds, zero bonds pay no interest until they mature. To make up for this, these bonds are sold at a deep discount. The interest, in a sense, turns into principal, which is paid to you in a lump sum at maturity. (You will still pay taxes along the way as though the bond does pay interest.) Zero coupon bonds are nice for college funding because you know exactly how much money you'll have when they mature. Since they lock in interest rates, unlike regular bonds, you will get a slightly lower yield.

Series EE bonds: If these bonds are owned by parents for at least five years and used for college tuition, they may be completely tax-deductible.

Prepaid college tuition plans: These plans allow you to pay for future college expenses at today's prices. You may, of course, be able to gain a much better return if you took the same amount of money and invested it wisely in the stock market, but these plans offer benefits. For one thing, you buy tuition in a state school at today's prices, and you are guaranteed that your investment will increase with the same rate as tuition (usually around 7 percent). These plans are offered by individual states, and most include a number of state schools to choose from, not just one.

Most prepaid plans also allow you to transfer the value of your contract to any accredited private or out-of-state public school, but you may face a penalty.

Uniform Gifts Minors Act (UGMA): You can

WALL STREET WISDOM: ***Asset allocation made easy:***

Asset allocation is a technical term that simply means how you divide your assets among different investment types—for example, stocks, bonds, and cash investments. Variety is the spice of life. In this case, it may also help to reduce your investing risk.

First, figure out your basic asset allocation *needs—the mix of stocks, bonds, and cash investments that best suits you—based on your long-term investment goals. What this means is that you consider what you need the money for—a new car, a new house, or a secure retirement—and structure your portfolio accordingly. In general, investors with longer time horizons are less vulnerable to market volatility.*

Asset allocation is a way to diversify. It's not the whole story, though. You can also diversify within an asset class. For example, the stock mutual fund portion of your portfolio may include aggressive growth funds, growth and income funds, and sector funds. If you want to use another cliché, asset allocation means not putting all your eggs in one basket.

As your goals change over time, so will your asset allocation. What else can affect the makeup of your portfolio? A shorter investment time frame; changes in your financial or tax situation; or a change in your risk tolerance.

Creating a solid asset allocation plan is like changing the oil in your car—subtle, but absolutely necessary. According to Ibbotson Associates, an investment counseling firm in Chicago, choosing the particular investments in your portfolio accounts for only around 10 percent of your investment performance. The other 90 percent will most likely be determined by how you allocate *your investment dollars.*

make investments in your child's name with these accounts. These are irrevocable gifts to the child made via custodial accounts—for example, through a custodial account at a mutual fund company. The custodian, an adult in the child's life, manages the fund until the minor is 18. The funds are taxed at the child's rate.

Q: What are Treasuries, when should I buy them, and where can I buy them?

A: The federal government carries an enormous amount of debt, and the American public is one of its largest lenders. In order to make up for the gap between what the government has and what it needs to work effectively, it borrows money through the U.S. Treasury The Treasury raises money through selling Treasury bills, notes, and bonds. When you buy these you are lending money to the government.

Treasuries are considered fixed-income investments, and are handy for the less risky portion of your portfolio. You can purchase Treasuries through any full-service broker or commercial bank. You can also purchase Treasuries directly from the Department of the Treasury and forgo handling charges. Ask for the Treasury Direct program.

Q: Where can I get more information on retirement planning?

A: Take advantage of the free educational brochures, magazines, and kits provided by mutual fund companies. T. Rowe Price, for example, offers two free kits—Retirement Planning Kit and Retirees Financial Guide. Call 800-541-8460.

Q: What's long-term care insurance, and when should I consider buying it?

A: Long-term care insurance covers extended health care for seniors that is not covered by Medicare, including nursing home care or adult day care. Long-term care insurance can preserve assets and ensure care in the case of an adult disability. Average annual premium costs are $1,200 per year. The earlier you buy the policy, the lower your rates, and the greater your chance for qualifying. Look for an inflation rider and a policy that's renewable for life.

WALL STREET WISDOM: ***How do you make sure that you don't make Uncle Sam your heir? Keep the following guidelines in mind when it comes to transferring money from one generation to the next.***

1. *You can give yearly gifts of up to $10,000, tax-free, to family members or others. The drawback is that you're giving away your money before your estate matures (which is a euphemism for "before you die"), but your family will get the money tax-free. That's a lot of savings.*
2. *If you use some of your money to pay your dependents' schooling or medical bills, you're also exempt from taxes.*
3. *Remember to update your life insurance. Let's say that your life insurance names your neighbor Harry as your beneficiary, because when you made your will he was the closest person to you. Now years have passed, you've married, and have a family. Even though your will may specify that all assets go to your dependents, unless you change that life insurance beneficiary designation—you guessed it—Harry gets the stash.*
4. *Give your beneficiaries your appreciable assets now (such as stocks), rather than in your will. Again, they will pay less taxes on the appreciation of the assets.*

Q: What is estate planning, and what do I need to take care of to protect my assets for my family?

A: A will is what most of us think of when we think of estate planning. A will is simply a legal document that dictates who will manage your estate, and who will get your property and belongings. You always want to have a current will; otherwise, when you die, you will die intestate, which means the state determines who gets what. It will even decide who will take care of your children.

Also consider getting a *durable power of attorney,* which hands over the management of your affairs to someone you trust in the event that you become disabled. Otherwise, your family might have to have a court-appointed guardian. This could result in delays, expense, and lack of privacy.

FYI: A *guardian* is the person responsible for the day-to-day well-being of your children following your death. The *trustee* is the person or institution that you've appointed to manage the assets.

Q: Why should I buy bonds, and should I buy individual issues or bond mutual funds?

A: Bonds, which provide fixed income, or a set amount of return, are for safety and stability in your investment portfolio. Buying bonds doesn't make sense unless you have at least $10,000 to invest. Bonds have high minimum investments; some begin at $25,000.

Your best bet may be to buy a bond mutual fund. The average municipal bond fund has over eighty holdings, so it offers diversity for less cost. You can share your mutual fund shares at any time. Muni-bond funds offer the advantages of any mutual fund—diversity, professional management, and accessibility. Bond funds are usually identified by the average maturity of the bonds that they hold. Long-term bond funds are the most volatile; they have to endure years of interest rate fluctuations. Short-term funds are more stable, but likely pay lower yields.

When you're looking for a bond fund, consider its investment objective, its expenses, and its record.

Q: How do I know what my credit record looks like? Why is this important?

A: Many credit reports contain errors, and the onus is on you to prove them erroneous and correct them. It always makes sense to have an idea of what yours looks like *before* you apply for credit, whether a mortgage, car loan, or school loan. The following are the big three of the credit bureaus. It's a good idea to order your credit report once a year.

Equifax: P.O. Box 740241, Atlanta, GA 30374-0241; 800-685-1111

Experian: P.O. Box 949, Allen, TX 75013; 800-682-7654

Trans Union: P.O. Box 390, Springfield, PA 19064; 800-916-8800

Q: I've made some poor credit moves in my past. Should I rely on a credit-repair company to fix my credit report?

A: Watch out for credit-repair scams. No matter what they claim, credit-repair firms cannot remove *accurate* information from your credit report. Federal law allows credit bureaus to report accurate credit history information for seven years, ten years for bankruptcies. You can fix the inaccurate information yourself for little or no charge.

WALL STREET WISDOM: ***Maintaining your investment portfolio: According to Dave Cox of the Chicago Trust company, here's what to do to preserve your financial portfolio.***

1. **Keep track of your investments.** *Review your portfolio periodically, perhaps once a year. Try to avoid doing this at year-end when hype is at its worse. Midyear may be a time when you can get a stronger focus. Mix it up throughout the year so that you get different perspectives.*
2. **Take a stable outlook.** *Don't make too many unnecessary changes either in assets or how they are allocated. Once you've created an effective portfolio, don't be too quick to jump ship. Of course, you'll consider selling when it's time for a big, planned purchase. In this type of situation, don't wait until the last minute to sell. The market could go against you, and you could wind up with less money than you were expecting.*

   You might want to sell, or to make changes if one asset class becomes too large, or if you see a consistent underperformance from one fund or asset. Also be on the lookout for a change in the characteristics of an investment, or if a company merges, or a mutual fund changes managers. These are all opportunities for evaluating whether to sell.

   Do not sell an investment just because it performs well. There's a tendency to take profits. If an investment is performing well because that's what it's supposed to do, that's probably a good investment to hold onto. Also, don't switch to something just because it's recently done well. Make smart choices and stick with them.
3. **Remember what your long-term goals are.** *Keep the big picture in mind. This can help when temptation calls. Try not to take your savings out except for major planned expenses.*
4. **Don't withdraw early from your tax-advantaged accounts.** *Not only are you risking big penalties but you're also interrupting your retirement investing.*

Q: What are Systematic Withdrawal Plans (SWPs), and when should I take advantage of these?

A: SWPs are basically the opposite of dollar-cost averaging. They're a handy tool if you're retired or want to use your mutual fund earnings to help pay mortgage payments, insurance premiums, or any other type of financial obligation. Instead of calling or writing your mutual fund for share redemptions, under a SWP you set up an automatic redemption of your shares. This redemption check can come directly to you, to a third party, or to your bank account.

Usually, you need to have a minimum in order to participate, sometimes from $5,000 to $10,000. Also, you need to commit to a minimum withdrawal every month, usually $50. You can have the money withdrawn every month, twice a month, or quarterly. The benefits are clear: Paperwork is reduced, and you're generating a steady stream of income. You can order the redemptions in dollar amounts, fixed number of shares, a fixed percentage, or declining balance based on your life expectancy.

Q: What financial records should I keep?

A: It's a good idea to keep records of all investment transactions (buying, selling, reinvesting). You are required to report all sales of taxable investments in a personal account to the IRS. You can do this through statements furnished by your mutual fund company, DRIP company, or brokerage company. Also, keep copies of records that show how much money has gone into investments, whether through automatic transfer, optional cash payment, or stock purchases.

Q: How do I keep track of my overall investing progress?

A: You want to keep track of what the value of your investments are compared to your projections. Are you ahead of the game? Lagging behind? You want to see if the value of your portfolio is growing, remaining the same, or decreasing. As your investments get more diverse and complicated, you may choose to use one of the many inexpensive financial software programs that are available.

Look at the big picture first, and then at each individual investment. Ask yourself if anything has changed in your life or feelings that will affect how you feel about risk and volatility. Depending on your answer, you need to take action. Look at each investment individually: Is each still valid for its category? Compare it to an index, such as the S & P 500, to see how it's performing. You can find indexes in the business section of newspapers or the financial press. For mutual funds, go to the library and read Morningstar or Value Line. Morningstar has an index and funds comparison. If you have a fund that's underperforming, find out why. If it's only been underperforming for a year, and the manager, support staff, or philosophy hasn't changed, put it on your watch list and wait it out another six months or a year. If a mutual fund dramatically underperforms, take more immediate action. Ask yourself the same thing about your retirement allocation: Have my goals changed? Have one of my investments underperformed? Look at how your retirement plan is affecting your overall portfolio. Remember, always think of your investments as an aggregate return. Make your tracking easier by identifying the records you must keep, and keeping those records in an organized place You want to save the phone numbers and addresses of all your investments; know the tax consequences of your investments; monitor the value of your holdings regularly; and keep track of your progress toward your goals.

Q: What are warning signs that I should consider selling a stock?

A: Consider selling a stock if you don't have enough confidence in the company to want to buy any more of its stock. What might tip you off? If the firm's revenue, profitability, return on capital, or market share deteriorates significantly; if the company's long-term debt is over 50 percent; or if serious legal action is being brought against a company. Watch, too, to see how management addresses these problems. If it clearly addresses its problems, that may be a reason to stick around for a while longer, but if it ignores them, that's another danger sign.

WALL STREET WISDOM: ***Rules of the Road: When you understand the basics of investing and can engineer a plan that works for you, you're headed in the right direction on Wall Street. Before you go, pack our top-ten tips for the $5-a-day investor.***

1. ***Pay yourself first.*** *When saving becomes a habit, you're starting off on the right foot. Often, finding the money to invest is merely a matter of shifting your priorities. Consider your saving and investing contributions as nonnegotiable as paying your mortgage, rent, or car loan.*
2. ***Build a solid foundation.*** *Before you invest, make sure that you've covered certain risks. Obtain life, health, and disability insurance. Create an accessible savings account for emergencies. When you've protected your assets, you're able to invest continu-*

ally over a long period of time without having to dip into your permanent portfolio for life's curveballs.

3. ***Create a time line that maps out your financial goals.*** *This enables you to know what types of investments to choose. It also helps you get what you want from your money—and life. After all, as the saying goes, if you don't know where you are going—you just might end up there.*
4. ***Take full advantage of retirement plans.*** *Retirement plans are one of the best deals around for the $5-a-day investor. At the very least, they offer you tax savings. You may also find that your retirement plan offers a matching feature. In these plans, not only is your taxable income reduced by what you contribute but the money that you* and *your employer contribute compounds tax-free.*
5. ***Take advantage of mutual funds.*** *Mutual funds allow the $5-a-day investor to get in the stock market easily and effectively. Mutual funds offer diversification, professional management, and accessibility. You have from over 7,000 to choose from; it's a good bet that you'll find several that meet your investment objectives and philosophy.*
6. ***Watch the loads and fees when you invest.*** *With the proliferation of no-load mutual funds and no-load stocks, there's little reason to spend your precious money on anything else but your investment. You want as much of your $5 a day going toward compound interest. Remember, every penny counts.*
7. ***Consider Dividend Reinvestment Plans (DRIPs) and investment clubs.*** *The $5-a-day investor has more options than ever before to make money on Wall Street. DRIPs allow you to buy individual stocks without high (or any!) brokerage fees, and investment clubs are a great means for disciplined investing.*
8. ***Take appropriate risks.*** *You've heard this a million times, but it's a handy mantra to have. One of the greatest risks of all is to play it too safe. Inflation grows at an average rate of 3 percent per year. If your assets can't keep up with this, you'll end up outliving them. The longer your time horizon, the more risks you can afford to take.*

Q: How do I know how much risk I can live with?

A: Your level of risk depends on several things—your investment time frame, your investment goals, your tolerance for risk, and your age. Time probably has the greatest impact on your risk tolerance. If your goals are far in the future, obviously you can afford to take more risk. For your immediate goals, it's a good idea to temper risk with security. The more time you have, the more fluctuation you can withstand. As always, playing it too safe brings with it its own risk: losing out on purchasing power. There's a very simple rule of risk, called the sleep rule. If it keeps you up at night, it's too risky for you.

Q: Is there an easy way to figure out how much money I need for retirement?

A: A general rule of thumb is that your retirement income should equal 75 percent of your pre-retirement take-home pay. For a pretty accurate projection of your retirement needs, take your current expenses and add or detract costs that will change in retirement. For example, you may have less financial obligations concerning children, education, or mortgage. You may have higher travel, medical, and home maintenance costs. When in doubt, assume a longer time in retirement, a higher rate of inflation, and a lower rate of return on your investments. Remember, too, that retirement is a nebulous concept. Many people will choose to continue to work long past "retirement" age.

Sources and References

Financial Newspapers

Investor's Business Daily
(Published Monday through Friday)
Investor's Daily, Inc.
1941 Armacost Avenue
Los Angeles, CA 90025
800-831-2525

The Wall Street Journal
(Published Monday through Friday)
Dow Jones & Company, Inc.
World Financial Center
200 Liberty Street
New York, NY 10281
800-568-7625

Financial Magazines

Barron's National Business & Financial Weekly
(Published weekly)
Dow Jones & Company, Inc.
PO Box 7014
Chicopee, MA 01020
800-544-0422

Business Week
(Published weekly)
McGraw-Hill, Inc.
1221 Avenue of the Americas
New York, NY 10020
800-635-1200

Forbes
(Published biweekly)
60 Fifth Avenue
New York, New York 10011
800-888-9896

Money
(Published monthly)
Time, Inc.
Time & Life Building
Rockefeller Center
New York, NY 10020
800-633-9970

Smart Money
(Published monthly)
Hearst Company and Dow Jones & Company
1790 Broadway
New York, NY 10019
800-444-4204

Your Money
8001 N. Lincoln Avenue
Sixth Floor
Skokie, Illinois 60077-3657
800-777-0025

Rating Services

Lipper Analytical Service Mutual Fund Profile
(Published quarterly)
Standard & Poor's Corporation
25 Broadway
New York, NY 10004
212-393-1300

Morningstar Mutual Fund Values
(Published biweekly)
Morningstar, Inc.
53 W. Jackson Blvd.
Chicago, Illinois 60604
800-735-0700

Value Line Mutual Fund Survey
(Published biweekly)
Value Line Publishing
711 Third Avenue
New York, NY 10017
800-284-7606

Value Line Investment Survey
(Published weekly)
Value Line Publishing
711 Third Avenue
New York, NY 10017
800-284-7606

Publications Relating Specifically to DRIPs

Buying Stocks without a Broker
Charles B. Carlson
McGraw-Hill
11 West 19th Street
New York, NY 10011
800-338-3987

The Moneypaper Guide to Dividend Reinvestment Plans
The Moneypaper
1010 Momaroneck Avenue
Mamaroneck, NY 10543
800-388-9993

Standard & Poor's Directory of Dividend Reinvestment Plans
Standard & Poor's Corporation
25 Broadway
New York, NY 10004
800-852-5277

Discount Brokers

Burke, Christensen & Lewis Securities, Inc.
303 West Madison Street
Chicago, Illinois 60606
800-621-0392

Fidelity Brokerage Services, Inc.
82 Devonshire Street
Boston, MA 02109
800-544-8888

Olde Discount Stock Brokers
910 3rd Avenue
Seattle, WA 98104
800-521-1111

Charles Schwab & Company
101 Montgomery Street
San Francisco, CA 94104
800-435-4000

USAA Brokerage Services
USAA Building
San Antonio, TX 78284-9859
800-531-8000

Jack White & Company
9191 Towne Center Drive
Suite 220
San Diego, CA 92122
800-233-3411

Online Brokers
DLJ Direct www.dljdirect.com
Web Street Securities www.webstreetsecurties.com
E*TRADE www.etrade.com
Waterhouse Securities www.webbroker.com
National Discount Brokers www.ndb.com

Glossary

American Stock Exchange: The second-largest stock exchange in the United States. Located in New York, its nickname is AMEX. It originally began as the New York Curb Exchange, because these lesser brokers were shunted to the curbside from the New York Stock Exchange. (When the AMEX was still the Curb Exchange, the hoity-toity NYSE folk fined their own members for behavior they thought un-brokerlike. Knocking off a member's hat was a 50 cent charge. Throwing a paper dart garnered a ten dollar penalty. I wonder what insider trading would have brought?)

Annuities: Long-term investments, usually with sales charges and early surrender fees. Annuities are contracts, sold usually by insurance companies but also by banks, that ensure periodic payments to the holder of the contract at a future date—usually starting at retirement. A fixed annuity pays a fixed rate, and a variable annuity pays whatever investment returns the annuity is invested in. An immediate-income annuity begins income payments right away. A deferred annuity can be fixed or variable and keeps your investment growing, shielded from taxes until you begin to withdraw the money.

Although annuities are often confused with life insurance—probably because insurance companies sell both—they are quite different. Think of annuities as providing you money while you live, and life insurance as providing money in the event of your death.

Asset allocation: A technical term that simply means how your investments are divided up—for instance, among stocks, bonds and cash investments. Studies indicate that 90 percent of an investment portfolio's performance is due to its asset allocation rather than when the investments were bought and sold. With a retirement portfolio, it's a good idea to keep up-to-date with your asset allocation. For example, the further away you are from retirement or accessing your money, the more you may consider investing in stocks. The closer you get to retirement, the more you may choose to move your investments into cash vehicles.

Asset class: A category of investments, such as stocks, bonds, or cash. When you allocate your assets, you divide your investments into different investment categories.

Automatic reinvestment: A great friend of compound interest. The mutual fund company automatically reinvests capital gains or dividend payments.

Barometers and indicators: How analysts, experts, neophytes, and anyone else anticipate what Wall Street is going to do, or where the market is going. Common indicators include the buying and selling of stocks by insiders—that is, top executives, directors, and large shareholders. There's also the January barometer, which asserts that January previews the year. The Super Bowl indicator shows the silliness of it all: The market seems to rise when a National Football League team wins. Basically, indicators can say anything, as can analysts.

Bear and bull markets: These terms describe the state of the stock market: Is it doing well, or is it ailing? In short, a bull market is a strong one, and a bull is someone who expects a rise in prices for a given investment—in other words, an optimist. A bear market is in decline, and a bear expects declining prices—a pessimist.

Controversy exists as to the origination of these terms. An easy explanation may be that a bull thrusts upward when attacking, while a bear paws downward. So, if you're bullish on the market, you're expecting good things. We're bullish on the idea of $5 a day.

Blue chips: Just like a blue chip in poker, this term means quality on Wall Street too. Specifically, a blue-chip stock is the stock of a successful, established company. Like a lot of Wall Street terms, however, it's relative. It may refer to a company included on the Forbes 500 list or a company that is well-established and steady. The definition may also be temporary; something may be a blue-chip stock today, but not tomorrow. Often stocks termed as blue chip do not anticipate wild growth. Rather, they can provide stability and income. Think establishment.

Bonds: A bond is basically an IOU. You, the lender, loan your money to an organization, whether government or public, at a set rate of interest. The borrower, or issuer, agrees to pay you back in full, at a specific rate of interest, by a specific date. Bonds range in safety, from the very safe U.S. government bonds to the high-risk but potentially high-reward junk bonds, which are bonds issued by start-up companies.

Capital gains distributions: Capital gains are the profits from the sale of an investment within a mutual fund. Mutual fund companies usually allow these to be automatically reinvested for no cost.

Capitalization: A company's total value based on its market price, the number of outstanding shares times the price of each share. Companies with large market value are called large cap stocks; those with small value are known as small caps. Small caps are usually under $1 billion in market capitalization. Mid-caps are usually between $1 billion and $3 billion.

Certificate of Deposit (CD): This bank deposit is a specific amount of money placed in an account for a fixed amount of time at a fixed rate of interest. You can obtain a CD for anywhere from several months to several years, in amounts ranging from several hundred dollars to thousands of dollars. Typically, CDs pay higher rates than regular bank accounts because you commit to keeping your money in for a specific length of time; you do not have the right to withdraw without penalty.

Common stock: Shares in a publicly held company. Although you're last man on the totem pole for dividend payments if you own common stock (bondholders and preferred stock owners are first), you get voting rights.

Compound interest: Interest on your interest. For instance, if your money is invested in an account that offers 10 percent interest compounded quarterly, you'll actually end up with more than a 10 percent return at the end of the year. At the first quarter, you'll receive an interest payment. After that point, your interest will be calculated off the new total. Simple interest, on the other hand, offers just the stated amount at the end of the year.

Convertible bond: A bond that can be traded in for stock at a specified price.

Correction: A correction is a nice way of saying a market loss of more than 10 percent—or a really bad day on Wall Street. A good example is the "correction" of 1990. The market typically goes through a correction every several years.

Coupon: A bond's interest rate. The name comes from the stub attached to the bond listing the amount of interest to be paid and the date it is to be paid.

Custodian: The financial institution that overlooks your investment assets and is responsible for their safekeeping.

Cyclical stocks: As an investor, you may hear this term a lot. A cyclical stock is one that is affected by cycles. Market cycles are inevitable—expansion followed by slowdown and then recovery to expansion again. Some stocks, and therefore mutual funds, are more affected by cycles than others. Examples of cyclical stocks include the housing industry, steel, paper, chemicals, and machine-tool and semiconductor stocks.

Defined-benefit plans: A pension that guarantees a certain amount of money to employees who have worked at a company for a set amount of time. In many of these plans, the employer makes the contributions and invests them for employees.

Defined-contribution plans: Also known as salary-reduction plans or employee-directed plans, these are the 401(k)s and 403(b)s that allow employees to contribute up to 10 percent of their salary before tax. They can choose from several different investment choices, but the performance of these investments, unless they choose guaranteed investment contract (GIC), which offer a fairly stable, though low, rate for a given period of time is not guaranteed. So the responsibility of contributing anything at all, and how the investments do, are the employee's.

Diversification: Investing in different types of investments so that you lessen the risk you take—in other words, not putting all your eggs in one basket. For a mutual fund investor, this would mean investing in different types of funds—say, a balanced fund, an aggressive growth fund, and an international fund—and across different fund families.

Dividend: A portion of a company's profit's paid out to you, the stockholder. As a company grows more profitable, so do its dividends. However, not all companies pay dividends. Dividends have become less popular because they are currently taxed at a taxpayer's highest marginal rate rather than the usually lower capital gains rate.

Dollar-cost averaging: One of the great tools for entering the stock market. Dollar-cost averaging is merely buying stocks or mutual funds in a consistent, systematic way over time. For example, signing up for $50 a month to be automatically deducted from your checking account into a mutual fund is dollar-cost averaging. You are investing set amounts of money at regular intervals. You buy more shares when prices are lower, and fewer shares when prices are higher, which results in a lower average price per share.

Dow-Jones averages: Some of the stock indexes, or daily average of stock prices on the New York Stock Exchange, used to gauge the performance of the stock market. Stock indexes tell investors which way stock prices are heading. The Dow-Jones industrial average is the most famous of the indexes.

Emerging growth stocks: Stocks of companies still in the early stages of development that have strong growth prospects. They offer the potential of both greater risk and greater reward. The same is true for an emerging growth stock mutual fund.

Employee-directed plans: See defined-contribution plans.

Expense ratio: Usually the best indication of a mutual fund's cost. The expense ratio is expressed as a percentage of the fund's assets, and includes management and 12b-1 fees, but not loads. The higher the expense ratio, the less the fund pays its shareholders. Fixed-income and index funds have the lowest expense ratios; smaller funds and international funds usually have the highest. In general, try to stay with funds with expense ratios under 1.5 percent.

Face value: The value printed or written on a bond or certificate of deposit. It is the amount you purchase the instrument for. For example, if you purchase a CD for $5,000, that's its face value. Face value does not include interest payments.

Federal Deposit Insurance Corporation (FDIC): A federal agency that insures investors' bank deposits. A bank or savings and loan association must take out insurance with the FDIC. Each depositor of the bank is insured for up to $100,000 should the bank fail.

Fixed-income investment: An investment that pays a set rate of interest, such as a bond, CD, or savings account. Since these investments generally are safer than non-fixed-income investments, such as stocks or stock mutual funds, the rate of return is usually less.

401(k) plans: Company sponsored retirement plans. Your contributions are tax-deferred and -deductible, and you have a choice of vehicles, usually stocks or stock funds, bond funds, or fixed-income investments. Some employers even match your contributions. It is one of the best ways to invest.

Guaranteed Investment Contract (GIC): These are contracts between insurance companies and corporate pension plans that offer a fixed rate of return over the life of the contract. Although these are not federally insured, they are usually less risky than stock options, although they may not keep up with inflation.

Income dividend: These are the payments that you'll periodically receive from a mutual fund reflecting the fund's interest earnings.

As with capital gains distributions, you can choose to have these automatically reinvested into your fund.

Index funds: These funds purchase the same stocks as those in a particular index—let's say the S & P 500, for example. The performance of the fund will then mirror the performance of the index. Investors can participate in the long-term growth of the market at a low cost. (There's less buying and selling in these funds so these funds don't require large research staffs—therefore so lower expense ratios.)

Individual Retirement Account (IRA): A self-directed retirement account in which an investor can place up to $2,000 per year. Available through banks, brokerage firms, mutual fund companies, and insurance companies, these accounts are tax deferred—you don't pay taxes on the money deposited or interest earned until you withdraw the money—if you are not offered a retirement plan at work or you earn under a certain amount of income. You generally cannot withdraw (without penalty, that is) money from your IRA until you are fifty-nine and a half years old.

IRA rollover: Allows employees to avoid taxes by transferring a lump-sum payment from a 401(k) or profit-sharing plan into an IRA within 60 days.

Inflation: An increase in the general cost of living. The result: you can buy less with your money.

Interest-sensitive stocks: As interest rates rise, they increase the yields available to new buyers of bonds. When interest rates fall, bonds become less attractive to new investment money. In theory at least, rising interest rates may discourage home building and buying as well as investing in new businesses.

A company that borrows large sums of money in its business

may depend on favorable interest rate conditions—for example, stocks of savings and loan holding companies. In addition, utilities, such as electric, gas, and telephone companies are interest sensitive because they are heavy users of borrowed money to finance capital expenditures.

Investment objective: Included in the fund's prospectus, this details what a mutual fund hopes to accomplish.

Junk bonds: Bonds issued by companies or organizations that are high risk—start-up companies, for example, or rated BBB or below by Moody's or Standard & Poor's. With the higher risk comes a higher potential for reward.

Keogh plan: Another type of self-directed retirement plan. This one is for self-employed persons. As eligible person can deposit up to 25 percent of his or her earnings—but no more than $30,000 per year—in a Keogh plan, which is available through a bank, brokerage firm, insurance company, or mutual fund company. Like an IRA, deposits and earnings are tax-deferred and tax-deductible. You can only withdraw your money (without penalty) after you reach age fifty-nine and a half.

Liquidity: The accessibility of your investment. A savings account is very liquid, because you can typically get your money at any time. Real estate is illiquid because it's less easily converted into cash.

Loads: Also known as commissions, this is what a broker or some mutual fund companies will charge you to invest in their fund. Your best bet is typically no-load funds, where all of your money is going toward your investment.

Mutual funds: A way for investors to pool their money and enter the stock market.

Net asset value: Also known as a mutual fund's share price.

New York Stock Exchange (NYSE): The largest and oldest stock exchange in the United States, founded in 1792. The NYSE is located at 11 Wall Street in New York City. The oldest and most established companies tend to trade on the NYSE.

Option: The right to buy or sell something on or before a future date at the price set at the time the option was granted.

Portfolio: Your investments. Your stocks, bonds, mutual funds, and other assets. Think of it as a nice little briefcase containing pictures of everything that you own for making and saving money.

Prime rate: The lowest rate of interest at which banks and other lending institutions will lend money. The prime rate will go up and down depending on economic conditions.

Prospectus: A printed summary of information about a mutual fund, which is also a registration statement filed with the Securities and Exchange Commission (SEC). According to SEC regulations, this will contain information that allows the consumer to make informed decisions about investing.

Salary-reduction plan: See defined-contribution plans.

Stock split: The adding of stock to a company by dividing each share of its present stock into two or more shares. Why are stocks split? So that companies can entice new stockholders with lower prices. When a stock has recently split, the letter S appears after the company name in the newspaper stock listings.

Tax-deductible: This means that the investment gets made with pretax dollars. In other words, you deduct the amount that you invest from your gross salary so that you pay less taxes. 401(k) and 403(b) plans are tax-deductible, as are some IRAs.

Tax-deferred: Exactly as the name implies, any tax-deferred investment defers, or postpones, paying taxes. Retirement plans are tax-deferred, which is a good thing because your money gets to grow without paying out of it for taxes on capital gains or dividends earned. This is not the same as tax-deductible. (See tax-deductible.) Nor is it the same as tax-exempt, which means that you never pay taxes on that particular investment.

Total return: You may invest in a stock or mutual fund for capital gains, when you earn money as the stock or mutual fund increases in worth, or income. Either way, the point of investing is to make money. Total return is a simple concept: it is both the capital gains and the income and tax benefits derived from an investment.

Treasury bill (T-bill): A short-term security from the U.S. Treasury Department, worth $10,000 or more, that pays interest. These bills end in three to six months, and the holder can buy another at that time. The Treasury Department borrows the money for government use.

Treasury bond: A long-term security issued by the U.S. Treasury Department that usually matures in five years or more. Minimum purchase is $1,000, and the interest rate is usually higher than it is with T-bills, because your money is tied up for a longer time.

Undervalued: In the eyes of the beholder, an undervalued stock is a bargain; an overvalued stock is a bad buy. Again, these are subjective terms. The only true value of a stock or mutual fund is the highest price someone is willing to pay.

Vested: When an employee is vested, he or she has earned the right to receive employer-contribution benefits. This usually happens after a specific period of time, and it can happen gradually. For example, Employee X may have been contributing to his 401(k) plan for four years; however, he may not be fully vested until seven years. Therefore, if he leaves his job, he is eligible for only 40 percent of the employer's contributions.

X or XD (Ex-dividend): When an X appears next to a stock in the stock lists, it means that the stock is about to pay a dividend. When the X appears next to a bond, it means that an investor who buys the stock at that time is not entitled to the dividend.

Zero coupon bond: A bond that makes no interest payments but rather produces a profit for investors by being sold at a discount. For example, you can buy a $20,000 zero coupon bond today for $15,000, receive no interest payments, but cash it in for its entire sum in ten years. Because the IRS makes you pay taxes on these as if you were receiving the interest all along, zeros make sense in a tax-advantaged account.

Index

Page numbers in italics indicate sidebars, charts, etc.

A

C

D

E

G

H

I

N

O

P

Q

R

T

U